THINKING CRITICALLY ABOUT ETHICAL ISSUES

FOURTH EDITION

VINCENT RYAN RUGGIERO

Professor Emeritus
State University of New York, Delhi

Mayfield Publishing Company
Mountain View, California
London • Toronto

Library of Congress Cataloging-in-Publication Data

Ruggiero, Vincent Ryan.
  Thinking critically about ethical issues / Vincent Ryan Ruggiero.
—4th ed.
    p.   cm.
  Includes bibliographical references and index.
  ISBN 1–55934–654–X
  1. Ethics.   I. Title.
  BJ1012.R82 1996
  170—dc20   96–7989
                                                                    CIP

Manufactured in the United States of America
10 9 8 7 6 5 4 3 2 1

Mayfield Publishing Company
1280 Villa Street
Mountain View, California 94041

Sponsoring editor, James Bull; production editor, Larisa North; manuscript editor, Joan Pendleton; cover designer, Susan Breitbard. The text was set in 10/13 Palatino by London Road Design and printed on 50# Butte des Mortes by Banta Book Group.

Cover art: Paul Schulenburg

 Printed on recycled paper.

To
Vincent V. Ruggiero, my father,
Filomena Ruggiero, my grandmother,
Francis and Michael Ruggiero, my uncles, and
Edith and Bernhard Theisselmann, my "extra parents,"
whose quiet lessons and example first introduced
me to the subject of this book.

PREFACE

No introductory textbook can do complete justice to the subject of ethics. The best it can do is to help students develop a basic competency in ethical analysis and acquire a measure of confidence in their judgment; it should also stimulate enough interest in the subject that they will want to continue learning about it, formally or informally, when the final chapter is completed and the course is over. Even that relatively modest aim is difficult to achieve. The author must strike the right balance between the theoretical and the practical, between breadth and depth of treatment, and between rigor and relevance, so that students are challenged but not daunted.

This book is based on several specific ideas about how that crucial balance is best achieved:

The emphasis should be on DOING ethics rather than on studying the history of ethics. This does not mean that students should not become familiar with historical developments and the contributions of great ethicists. It means that more attention should be given to applying ethical principles to specific cases; that is, to conducting ethical analysis. This approach, which Alfred North Whitehead termed an emphasis on principles rather than details (and which he proposed as the standard for all education), is the same approach that many educators are recommending to promote the development of critical thinking skills in philosophy, the social sciences, and the humanities.

Careful attention should be given to overcoming students' intellectual impediments to ethical analysis. Today's students have been exposed to numerous misconceptions about ethical analysis—indeed, about thinking in general. For example, it is fashionable today to regard all value judgments as undemocratic. This fashion has led many students to the belief that whatever one *feels* is right is by that very fact right. Even when they manage to avoid that notion, many students adopt other erroneous notions—for instance, that the majority view is necessarily the best view or that morality is a religious matter only, without any secular dimension. Unless students get beyond such crippling notions, their efforts at ethical analysis are unlikely to be effective and meaningful.

The fundamental concerns in ethical analysis should be presented first, and more complex concerns reserved, wherever possible, until later. This may seem too obvious to state. Yet it is a consideration that many textbooks in ethics ignore. Such textbooks present a concept in detail, with all the conflicting interpretations of it that have been advanced by various ethical schools. This conflicting information can paralyze students' efforts. Instead of applying the concept in their work, as the authors intend, students often think, "If the experts disagree, how can I be expected to make sense of this?" The time for identifying complexities is after students have been introduced to the basic concepts and have become comfortable applying them in their analyses.

□ SPECIAL FEATURES OF THIS BOOK

The influence of the foregoing ideas accounts for certain features that distinguish this book from other texts. The most significant of these features are the following:

ORGANIZATION

The history of ethics and the contributions of great ethicists are presented at the end of the book (in Chapter 12) rather than at the beginning or throughout. This arrangement reflects the author's experience that most introductory students learn ethical analysis better when they are not burdened with names and dates and details of ethical systems. Showing students how Plato, Kant, and Mill approached an ethical issue and then asking them to analyze an issue themselves is very much like showing them a professional athlete performing and then saying, "Now, let's see how you perform." Both situations are intimidating; students are put in a competitive situation in which they cannot compete. In ethics, as in sports, it is better to postpone introducing students to "the professionals" until they have gained a little experience and confidence.

This format does not diminish the importance of ethical history. On the contrary, students are better able to appreciate and remember historical contributions after they have grappled with problems themselves and pondered the question of how to judge them. (In cases where course syllabi require that historical material be presented first, instructors can begin with Chapter 12 and then proceed with Chapters 1, 2, and so on.)

CHAPTER LENGTH

Short chapters allow students to spend less time reading and underlining and more time analyzing ethical problems. More conscientious students gain an additional benefit from the brevity of the chapters. These students are able to read each chapter more than once and thereby master the material better than they would with a long chapter.

APPENDIX ON WRITING

Today's students often arrive at college without the English proficiency that instructors expect them to have. The guide to writing included in this text can save instructors time and effort. Instead of trying to teach rhetorical skills during class or in conferences with students, instructors need only direct students to the Appendix. Students, too, benefit by being able to break the common cycle of submitting poor papers, getting poor grades, becoming frustrated, losing interest, and blaming the instructor. By knowing what is expected in their analyses of issues and, more important, how to provide it, they can devote more attention to the mastery and application of ethical principles.

The correction symbols noted in the Appendix can be used to make the evaluation of papers faster and more effective. If a paper is lacking in both coherence and development, the instructor need write nothing more than COH and DEV. Students will be able to turn to the appropriate sections of the Appendix, see what errors they have committed, and note how to avoid those errors in the future.

□ CHANGES IN THE FOURTH EDITION

In preparing the fourth edition I have been guided by the suggestions of a number of instructors who have used previous editions. The most significant of the changes are as follows:

- Section I, "The Context," has been streamlined so that students can more quickly understand the deficiencies of several popular perspectives on ethics. It now consists of five rather than six chapters. In addition, "Comparing Cultures" has been expanded to cover multiculturalism and has been repositioned; it now appears after, rather than before, the chapters on majority view, feelings, and conscience.

- In Section II a new chapter, "A Foundation for Judgment," has been added before the chapter on judgment criteria. It addresses a question that has challenged ethicists for centuries—is it possible to get from *is* to *ought*, from factual knowledge to moral norms? The chapter also discusses organizational codes of ethics, introduces the principle of right desire and the principle of contradiction, and helps students avoid the polar extremes of absolutism and relativism.

- Chapter 9, "Considering Ideals," and Chapter 10, "Considering Consequences," have been judiciously expanded.

- The chapter on errors in moral reasoning has been deleted and its contents included in various other chapters, notably Chapter 7.

- Sample responses have been added to early chapters to help students understand what is expected of them in the way of analysis. Also, new, timely exercises have been added in various chapters.

□ STANDARD FORMAT VS. ALTERNATIVES

The standard format is based on the author's experience that investing sufficient time to overcome misconceptions and build a sound philosophical perspective pays dividends in student learning. This format entails following the chapter order at a fairly leisurely pace, with more time devoted to examining the inquiries and forming/sharing judgments than to reading. Accordingly, in a fifteen-week semester course, approximately one week would be spent on each chapter, perhaps slightly more than that on Chapters 6–10. In this format enough time would remain for students to do an extended analysis of one or maybe two issues from "Contemporary Ethical Controversies."

For any one of several good reasons, of course, an instructor may wish to adjust this format. The following adaptations can be made with relative ease:

ALTERNATIVE 1

Situation: Students have already had some training in critical thinking and, in the instructor's view, will be able to master the material in Section I relatively quickly.

Approach: Devote one class period and one homework assignment to each chapter in Section I—that is, to each of Chapters 1–5. Allocate the remaining thirteen weeks to Chapters 6–12 and "Contemporary Ethical Controversies."

ALTERNATIVE 2

Situation: Students have already had *considerable* training in critical thinking or have otherwise achieved an unusual level of intellectual sophistication.

Approach: Make Chapters 1–5 *a single reading assignment,* with either no inquiries or only a few selected ones. Devote the remainder of the course to Chapters 6–12 and "Contemporary Ethical Controversies," focusing on individual and/or group analysis and discussion of the inquiries, perhaps involving the preparation of a term paper and/or formal debates toward the end of the course.

ALTERNATIVE 3

Situation: In the instructor's judgment, giving students an historical perspective at the outset of the course will enhance the learning experience.

Approach: Have students read Chapter 12, "A Perspective on History," and address its inquiry at the very beginning of the course. Then proceed with the other chapters, following the standard format or one of the other alternatives.

☐ A NOTE ON STUDENT FRUSTRATION

The approach used in the early chapters of this book will be frustrating to some students. They will ask, "If it's not feelings and not majority opinion that decide the morality of an action, then what is it? Why doesn't the author tell us?" This reaction is a reflection of students' prior classroom conditioning. They expect textbooks to provide neat answers that can be swallowed and then regurgitated on a test. When asked to think, to reason out for themselves the best answers to moral problems, they naturally become anxious for a time. The activity is unfamiliar.

Whenever your students ask, "What *does* decide the morality of an action?" you will know that their minds have become engaged in the subject, that they are seeing the need for a standard, other than feelings, for example, and are struggling to define it. By the time the book suggests the criteria of judgment (Chapter 7), students will be ready to learn and apply those criteria. Many, in fact, will already have anticipated the criteria in their own analyses of problems. Without realizing it, they will have been *doing* ethics.

□ ACKNOWLEDGMENTS

I am grateful to all who had a part in the making of this book. Special thanks go to Mary Ann G. Cutter, University of Colorado at Colorado Springs; Elaine E. Englehardt, Utah Valley State College; Beth Fitzsimmons, Loomis Chaffee School; Geoffrey Frasz, Community College of Southern Nevada; Aidan Gara, SUNY Delhi; Robert M. Giambattista, Cazenovia College; Linda S. Kayes, Oakland Community College; John M. Marran, Delaware County Community College; and Dianne S. Metzar, Broome Community College, for their helpful suggestions for revising the manuscript. Thanks also go to Jim Bull and Larisa North for directing the preparation of this new edition, and to Joan C. Pendleton for copyediting the manuscript.

Vincent Ryan Ruggiero

CONTENTS

Why do we need ethics? We have laws to
protect people's rights. We have religious
beliefs to guide their actions. If the laws
are enforced and the beliefs followed,
what need have we of further rules?

Is the basis for deciding moral values the
majority view? In other words, if the
majority of the citizens of our country
should decide that a particular action
is right, would that very decision
make the action right?

CHAPTER 7
THE BASIC CRITERIA   71

What is really good for us? What criteria
and approaches are most effective in
examining moral issues? What pitfalls
other than Relativism and Absolutism
should we be aware of and strive to avoid?

CHAPTER 8
CONSIDERING OBLIGATIONS   90

What do we do in situations where there
is more than a single obligation? How can
we reconcile conflicting obligations?

CHAPTER 9
CONSIDERING IDEALS   101

How can we reconcile conflicts
between ideals or between an ideal
and an obligation?

CHAPTER 10
CONSIDERING CONSEQUENCES   113

How do we deal with cases in which the
consequences are not neatly separable
into good and bad, but are mixed?

CHAPTER 11
DETERMINING MORAL RESPONSIBILITY   125

How do we determine whether a person is
responsible for her or his immoral actions?
Are there degrees of responsibility?

III / THE TRADITION

CHAPTER 12
A PERSPECTIVE ON HISTORY   **137**

When did the study of ethics begin? Who
were the great thinkers in the history of
ethics? What contributions did they make?

IV / CONTEMPORARY ETHICAL CONTROVERSIES

THE SAME MORAL ISSUES that men and women have grappled with throughout history have grown ever more complex in a society whose structures and forms are changing. And the impressive advances of science and technology have created a host of new issues.

Yet precisely at this time, when we most need a firm intellectual foundation to guide our judgment, we are confused by countless challenges to old and familiar faiths and standards.

The outlines of our very humanity are blurred by conflicting theories.

This, then, is the moral imperative of our time—to break the bonds of indecision, move beyond fad and foolishness, and address the dilemmas of modern living sensitively and sensibly, with regard for their complexity.

I

THE CONTEXT

CHAPTER ONE

THE NEED FOR ETHICS

Why do we need ethics? We have laws to protect people's rights. We have religious beliefs to guide their actions. If the laws are enforced and the beliefs followed, what need have we of further rules?

- A car speeds through a red light at a crowded intersection; a squad car begins pursuit, lights flashing and siren screaming.
- Two men are fighting in a bar; one pulls a knife, stabs the other, and runs out; the proprietor calls the police, who seek out the assailant.
- A store owner arrives at her place of business one morning and finds it has been burglarized; she reports the burglary, and detectives begin searching for clues to the burglar's identity.

Such events are unfortunately common. And there is nothing strange or unusual about the behavior of the police in response to them. In each case a law has been broken, and the police are doing their job—investigating the details of the case and apprehending suspects.

If asked where the laws came from, we would have little difficulty answering. They are made by legislators, "lawmakers," at various levels of government: local, state, national. But if we were asked what the legislators based those laws on, we might have more difficulty answering. Why did they prohibit speeding through red lights, stabbing others, and breaking into others' places of business and taking their property? The answer we would undoubtedly be driven to, after experiencing the frustration of groping for a more definitive response, is "Because those actions are wrong!"

With such cases, that answer would usually be satisfactory. Not so in all cases, however. Why can't a wage earner choose not to file an income tax return or use a different tax schedule from the one provided on the government form? Why can't people grow marijuana in their backyards or use crack cocaine in the privacy of their own homes? To say one can't perform these actions because they are wrong is not enough, for the question that leaps forth from that response is "But *why* are they wrong?" (if, indeed, they are wrong). To answer that question we must do something more than invoke the laws themselves. We must examine the moral perspective that underlies them.

If the laws themselves were a trustworthy measure of the rightness of actions, then there could not be a bad law. Every law would of necessity be just. Yet we know that some laws, or applications of laws, are unjust despite the good intentions of lawmakers. That is, they punish behavior that does not deserve punishment, or they make unreasonable demands. The Eighteenth Amendment to the U.S. Constitution made Prohibition the law of the land . . . until the Twenty-first Amendment repealed it in the name of justice. Members of the Amish religious sect, whose way of life called for less formal schooling than the law prescribed, were judged criminals for withdrawing their children from school . . . until the U.S. Supreme Court declared the application of the law to them unjust. In New York State, rape victims were required to prove they had given "earnest resistance" to the rapist . . . until the state legislature removed that unreasonable provision from the law.[1]

Laws are, in large part, a reflection of a country's conclusions about right and wrong. Such conclusions are separate from the law and precede it. They are not fixed and immutable, but alive and growing, changing as imperceptibly as our culture changes, responding to its challenges. They provide us all, including legislators and jurists, with a perspective from which to evaluate and classify actions, approving some and disapproving others.

□ ETHICS DEFINED

Ethics is the study of right and wrong conduct. In the scientific sense, it is a descriptive discipline, involving the collection and interpretation of data on what people from various cultures believe, without any consideration for the appropriateness or reasonableness of those beliefs. In the philosophical sense, the sense that concerns us, ethics is a two-sided discipline. One side, *normative ethics*, answers specific moral questions, determining what is reasonable and therefore what people should believe. (The term *normative* means setting "norms" or guidelines.) The other side of philosophical ethics, *metaethics,* examines ethical systems to appraise their logical foundations and internal consistency.

The focus of ethics is moral situations—that is, *those situations in which there is a choice of behavior involving human values* (those qualities that are regarded as good and desirable). Thus whether we watch TV at a friend's house or at our own is not a moral issue. But whether we watch TV at a friend's house without his or her knowledge and approval is a moral issue. Similarly, filling out an application for a job is a morally neutral act. But deciding whether to tell the truth on the application is a moral decision. An ethicist observes the choices people make in various moral situations and draws conclusions about those choices. An ethical system is a set of coherent ideas that result from those conclusions and form an overall moral perspective.

Ethicists are not lawmakers. They are neither elected nor appointed. Their only authority is the force of reasonableness in their judgments. Their words, unlike those of lawmakers, do not prescribe what must or must not be done. They merely suggest what *ought* to be done. If people violate their own or their society's moral code, no ethics enforcement officer will try to apprehend them—though if their action also violates a law, a law enforcement agency may do so.

Law enforcement, of course, extends beyond apprehension of alleged criminals. It includes the formal trial and judgment of guilt or innocence. There are, of course, degrees of guilt. A person who carries out a carefully planned murder is charged with a more serious crime than is a person who strikes and kills another in spontaneous, blind rage. In fact, if the individual in the latter case is judged to have been insane, he or she may go entirely unpunished.

The idea of varying degrees of responsibility for one's actions is applied in ethics, too. Although there are no courts of ethics as there are courts of law, and no formal pronouncements of guilt or innocence in moral matters, the ethicist nevertheless is interested in the question, "Under what circumstances is a person to be considered culpable?" (The conclusions ethicists reach in these matters provide guidance to lawmakers and law enforcers.)

☐ ETHICS AND RELIGIOUS BELIEF

Somehow the idea has arisen that ethics and religion are unrelated and incompatible. Thus when religious thinkers discuss ethical issues, especially in the context of political policy, they are thought to be exceeding their reach and perhaps even committing an offense against the principle of separation of church and state. How ironic that such a notion should arise at a time when popular culture no longer values the distinction between informed and uninformed opinion! In any case, the notion is without historical basis. In fact, an interesting case can be made for ethics having *originated* in religion. G. K. Chesterton, for example, argued as follows:

> Morality did not begin by one man saying to another, "I will not hit you if you do not hit me"; there is no trace of such a transaction. There is a trace of both men having said, "We must not hit each other in the holy place." They gained their morality by guarding their religion. They did not cultivate courage. They fought for the shrine, and found they had become courageous. They did not cultivate cleanliness. They purified themselves for the altar, and found that they were clean.[2]

Throughout our civilization's history, religious thinkers have spoken to the larger society on moral issues, and society has generally profited from their guidance. Problems arise only when religious leaders go beyond speaking *to* society and begin speaking *for* it on the basis of their particular theology. To be productive, ethical discourse must take place on common ground; that is, using understandings and intellectual procedures and judgment criteria that all participants—Christians, Jews, Moslems, atheists, and others—affirm. Because theology depends to a great extent upon faith, it does not provide that common ground. To say this is not to disparage theology but merely to acknowledge that it is not the tool for the job in question.

A focus on faith rather than reason can also prevent us from presenting the most persuasive ethical argument. A case in point is the controversy that arose some years ago over a National Endowment for the Arts (NEA) grant. It was awarded to artist Andres Serrano, who produced a work titled "Piss Christ," which consisted of a crucifix in a bucket of urine. Christians, believing that Jesus Christ is the Son of God, would understandably think Serrano guilty of blasphemy and the NEA guilty of supporting and approving the offense. But that charge would be ineffective as a *moral* argument offered to the general public. No matter how tasteless Jews, Moslems, atheists, and agnostics may have found Serrano's work, they are not likely to be persuaded that ridiculing a religious belief constitutes an ethical violation. A more persuasive argument is that the use of *tax dollars* for such work is immoral because it requires Christian citizens to contribute to the blatant disparagement of their religion.

Similarly, when speaking with those who do not share our religious views, it is not very helpful to judge actions by the criterion of whether they "please or offend God." The question that naturally arises is "How do you know whether they do or not?" And the two most common answers serve more to close off ethical inquiry than to promote it: One is "Because the Bible (or Koran, and so forth) says so." The other is "This is my religious belief." If we wish to pursue the matter further, we are placed in the position of having to challenge the Bible or to invade the very private domain of the other person's religious belief.

In addition, both answers are based on erroneous notions. Saying "the Bible says so" suggests that the Bible is a simple book that has a single interpretation. Yet biblical scholarship clearly demonstrates that it is complex and open to numerous interpretations. Saying "this is my religious belief" implies that no aspect of a person's belief can be shallow or mistaken, that in religious matters there is no room for growth and development. The lives of the saints and holy men and women of the world's religions disprove any such notion.

Some ethical questions cannot be adequately answered by reference to religious beliefs alone. Take, for example, the case of a person's wrestling with this question: "Since I no longer accept some of the major teachings of the church I was raised in, is it morally right for me to remain a member? What should I do?" The question is by no means an easy one, though it may appear so. Whatever approach the individual might use in answering it, the teachings of his or her religion would hardly be the definitive measure, for they are an integral part of the question. *Using those teachings would be equivalent to affirming them and closing the issue.*

Most religious thinkers recognize the error of judging moral issues merely by religious belief. They realize the importance of discussing them in a way that is meaningful and appealing to all people of goodwill and honest concern, a way that not only expresses their understanding of human behavior, but tests it and helps it to expand. For this reason, they distinguish carefully between religious belief and religious ethics. Religious ethics is the examination of moral situations from a particular religious perspective. In it, the religious doctrine is not a substitute for inquiry. It is a starting point, a guide to inquiry and to organizing the findings of inquiry.

□ THE NEED FOR ETHICS

Some people would have us believe that we don't need ethics because we have laws and religious beliefs. In reality, it is because of ethics (moral reasoning) that we have laws in the first place, and we continue to need ethics to refine and perfect our legal system. We also need ethics in order to discuss the practical implications of our religious beliefs with others who do not share those beliefs. In addition, in situations where the reasonableness of a particular belief is at issue, we need ethics to help us reach a sound decision. Three actual cases will dramatize the need for ethics.

The religion known as Voodoo, which originated thousands of years ago in Africa, is still practiced in some parts of the world by as many as 275 million people. It has a number of adherents in the United States, mainly in New York City, Miami, and New Orleans. Most of these adherents are black and Hispanic; some are white. Religious practices of Voodoo, known as Santeria in the United States, no longer include human sacrifice, but they do include animal sacrifice and the casting of spells with the aid of dolls or figurines. Some years ago, a farmer's field in upstate New York was the site of such a ritual. Four Voodoo dolls were found mutilated, and the area was littered with the bloody remains of a number of chickens, pigeons, lambs, and goats. Some of the animals and birds appeared to have had their heads *bitten off.*[3] Since the ritual was religious, it cannot effectively be objected to on religious grounds (except by saying, "My religious views make me deplore that religious practice"). And it may have broken no law, so the only legal objection may be "There *ought to be* a law." But on what basis ought there to be (or not be) a law? On the basis of moral judgment. Ethics.

The second example occurred in Minden, Louisiana. Because of their religious belief that God heals illness, a couple sought no medical help for their infant granddaughter, who was suffering from meningitis. When she died, they were arrested and charged with negligent homicide. A jury found them guilty.[4] In this case, the law and religious belief directly clash. If the law were the final arbiter of right and wrong, it would be impossible (or at least pointless) to discuss the case further. Yet we can discuss it further, can dispute whether the law is defensible and whether the decision in this case served justice. Whatever our position may be, it will be a product of ethical judgment.

The third example concerns a Santa Cruz, California, street clown known as Mr. Twister, who got into trouble with the law. As he walked about the downtown area in his clown costume, complete with painted face, a brightly colored wig, and a bulbous red nose, he would look for parking meters with time expired. When he found one, he would insert a quarter, often just before the meter maid arrived to issue a citation. Alas, his "random acts of kindness" violated a city ordinance against putting coins in the meter for another person. When the case was publicized, however, not only was the charge dismissed, but the City Council also decided that the ordinance criminalized the virtue of kindness and so repealed it.

Ethics fills an even more basic need in helping us interpret everyday human actions and decide what actions we approve in others and want to emulate ourselves. Will we go to work or call in sick? Follow the research protocol or violate it? Put quotes around borrowed phrasing or pretend the words are our own? Answer a colleague's question truthfully or lie? Obey the traffic laws or violate them? Pay bills on time or spend the money on entertainment instead? Respond to our spouse's need for appreciation and affection or ignore it? Ethics can help us find answers to such questions.

□ PRELIMINARY GUIDELINES

Later chapters will develop the guidelines that are necessary to reach thorough, thoughtful ethical judgments. But you will find it useful to have a preliminary approach to use in the meantime. The basic problem you will encounter is the tendency to judge issues on the basis of preconception and bias rather than careful analysis. Few people are completely free from the inclination to prejudgment on at least some issues. Some people may have their answer ready for any question concerning war; others, for questions concerning private property; still others, for issues involving alcohol or drugs. And many will have answers ready for questions of sexual morality. The reasons for prejudging will vary—from traumatic experience to personal preference to simple opinion. The underlying attitudes may range from distrust of all regulations, all laws, even all *thoughts,* to an uncritical endorsement of all traditions. But in each case the effect is the same: to avoid thinking about the particular case at all and merely to call forth a prefabricated, all-purpose answer.

The alternative to the closed mind is not the empty mind, however. Even if we wished to set aside completely all our prior conclusions about human behavior and right and wrong, we could not do so. The mind cannot be manhandled that way. Nor should it be. We can expect, then, that a flood of impressions and reactions will rush in upon our thoughts when we consider a moral issue. It is not the fact of that flood that matters, nor its force. It is what we do to avoid having our judgment swept away by it. Here are some suggestions:

1. *Be aware of your first impressions. Note them carefully.* Knowing the way your thinking inclines is the first step toward balancing it (if it needs balancing).

2. *Consider other views and the arguments that could be used to support them.* The position that directly opposes your first impression is often the most helpful one to consider. If your impression is wrong, this step will help you find out. If it is not, then you can return to it with confidence and present it more effectively for having considered alternatives to it.

3. *Keep your thinking flexible.* Do not feel obligated to your early ideas. The process of ethical thinking entails entertaining many ideas, some of which you will accept, some of which you will discard as inferior. No judgment is your "official" judgment until you endorse it publicly in speaking or writing, and even then you may choose to revise it. So change your mind as often as you like as you analyze an issue. The more fully and unprejudicially you explore the issue, the better your judgment is likely to be.

4. *Express your judgment precisely and explain the reasoning that underlies it.* It is all too easy to say something you don't quite mean, especially when the issue is both complex and controversial. The best way to avoid this problem is to experiment with several different ways of expressing your judgment instead of accepting the first version you produce. If your judgment is not a simple "yes" or "no," but a form of "it depends," be sure to specify what it depends on and exactly how your judgment would vary in different circumstances. Finally, no *statement* of your judgment is sufficient by itself. Be sure to explain, in as much detail as necessary for understanding, *what line of reasoning leads you to that conclusion rather than to some other one.*

⊞ SAMPLE RESPONSES

Here are two sample responses to help you understand the kind of analysis and the form of response appropriate for the inquiries that follow. (You need not agree with the particular viewpoints expressed.) Note that the responses express not just the writers' moral judgments but also the reasoning that underlies those judgments.

Inquiry: A Vestal, New York, resident unwittingly paid sewer bills for more than $1300 over an eighteen-year period and then discovered there was no sewer line connected to his home. Since the statute of limitations on civil suits of this kind is six years, the town attorney suggested that the man be reimbursed for six years of payments only.[5] Was this decision ethical?

Sample Response: *Having a time limit for filing may be reasonable in disputes about the quality or punctuality of a service. In such cases the passing of time could make the merits of the claim difficult to determine. A time limit might also make sense where each side was partly at fault. But this case is different. No service was provided and the town was completely at fault for the improper billing. The man should have received full reimbursement.*

Inquiry: Some coaches of nationally ranked college athletic teams are paid large sums of money by athletic shoe manufacturers for having their teams wear a particular brand of shoe. Is this practice ethical? Why or why not?

Sample Response: *It is my understanding that coaches of nationally ranked teams receive generous salaries from their institutions, so they can't be accepting the money because of economic need. They're using their positions to make a quick buck in the form of a bribe. Given that fact, it is likely that the shoe contract will go to the highest bidder, regardless of the quality of that company's shoes. I believe it is unethical for payment to be offered or accepted in this case.*

▨ INQUIRIES

If you need assistance composing your response, read "Writing About Moral Issues" in the Appendix.

1. When a Michigan man was arrested for soliciting a prostitute, the car he was driving was confiscated by the police in accordance with a local ordinance. His wife, who was co-owner of the vehicle, took the matter to court, claiming that the government's action was improper because it punished not only her husband but also her, even though she had no part in, or knowledge of, the crime he committed.[6] Was her argument morally sound? Explain.

2. The National Collegiate Athletic Association (NCAA) has no rule against colleges and universities making hundreds of thousands of dollars from the sale of tickets and television rights to games. Yet the NCAA does not permit colleges and universities to pay student athletes. Is the NCAA's position morally justifiable? Explain.

3. Although Maude is not physically handicapped, whenever she is in a hurry she parks her car in spaces reserved for the handicapped. Is she behaving unethically?

4. A village on the seacoast places restrictions on the use of its beaches. Residents of the village are issued beach passes for themselves and their guests. All others are barred. Is such a restriction a moral issue? That is, is it debatable in terms of right and wrong? Explain.

5. There is no legal obligation for an eligible voter to vote in an election in the United States. Is the decision to vote or not to vote a moral decision? Explain.

6. Certain people have spoken out against the American government's foreign and domestic policies. They have broken no laws. Their protests have been fully within the guarantees of free speech. Yet the FBI is directed to investigate each individual thoroughly. The FBI conducts background studies, including interviews with relatives, friends, and acquaintances. Are these investigations ethically justifiable? Explain.

7. A married couple, both addicted to drugs, are unable to care for their infant daughter. She is taken from them by court order and placed in a foster home. The years pass. She comes to regard her foster parents as her real parents. They love her as they would their own daughter. When the child is 9 years old, her natural parents, rehabilitated from drugs, begin court action to regain custody. The case is decided in their favor. The child is returned to them, against her will. Does ethics support the law in this case? Discuss.

8. A sociology professor spots a magazine article that will fit in well with the textbook chapter he has assigned his students. However, copyright law forbids his making copies of it without obtaining the publisher's or author's permission (usually given for a small fee). Since he cannot use college funds for this purpose, and since there isn't sufficient time to go through the process of obtaining permission, he decides to break the law and make the copies. Does he act rightly? Explain.

9. Zoo officials in Eureka, California, could not afford to house two healthy adult bears while a new bear grotto was being built, and the only other zoo that would take the bears was in South Dakota. Since the zoo could not afford the $500 it would have cost to transport the bears, officials decided to destroy them. As their two 3-month-old cubs looked on, the bears were given lethal shots of sodium phenobarbital.[7] Was the bears' destruction a moral issue? If so, was the action morally wrong?

10. Lawrence Steubig stole six candy bars in 1941. He was judged incompetent to stand trial and was sent to a mental institution. He was freed in 1975, *thirty-four years* later, whereupon he sued officials at the institution for "loss of liberty and loss of enjoyment of life." The institution could produce no records to show that he had ever received therapy or a chance to prove his competency. The judge ruled that Steubig's Fourteenth Amendment rights had been violated, but that he was not entitled to collect damages because the officials of the institution had acted in good faith.[8] Is this verdict defensible on moral grounds?

11. In November 1981, a Milpitas, California, boy raped and then killed his girlfriend and dumped her body in a lovers' lane gully. Over the next few days, the killer boasted to his high school friends and the word quickly spread that the girl was dead and that her body was in the gully. Carload after carload of high school students visited the gully to see the body. Some students prodded it with sticks or kicked it; one girl ripped a decal from the dead girl's jeans. Only one boy reported the murder to the high school principal, and even after the police investigation was well under way, only two students would identify the killer or volunteer any information. Since failure to report a body or to volunteer to testify is not a crime, the students could not be charged legally. But was the behavior of any of the students morally objectionable?

CHAPTER TWO

THE ROLE OF THE MAJORITY VIEW

Is the basis for deciding moral values the majority view? In other words, if the majority of the citizens of our country should decide that a particular action is right, would that very decision make the action right?

We live in an age when statistics confront us at every turn. From the moment we arise, authoritative voices bombard us with percentages. "Sixty-seven point two percent of the American public support the President's tax program." "Seven out of ten doctors recommend No-Ouch tablets." "My group had 90 percent less underarm odor."

In addition, tabloid television shows solicit our opinion on the issues of the day—"To vote YES, dial 1-900-555-2345. To vote NO, dial 1-900-555-5678." Verdict aside, did O. J. *really* commit the murders? Was more than one person involved in the assassination of Prime Minister Rabin? Should General Powell have run for the presidency? Tomorrow we'll learn how many people voted, and the official tally of their votes will be presented in the manner of sports scores. And we'll be tempted to believe that whichever side got the higher percentage won the contest.

Given a steady diet of such data, we may begin to believe that the majority view is the wisest, most informed view. But what, after all, is the "majority"? Nothing more than 51 percent or more of the *individuals* in a group. Although the conversion of a bunch of individual views into a statistic can create the impression of authoritativeness and wisdom, those qualities do not always result. *There is no magic in majorities.*

If we were to examine a particular majority and compare their individual thinking on a particular issue, what would we find? First, we would find that actual knowledge of the issue varied widely among the individuals. Some would be well informed about all details. Others would be completely uninformed, yet unaware of their ignorance. Between these extremes would be the largest group: those partly informed and partly ignorant, in some ways perceptive but in other ways confused or mistaken.

Second, we would find significant variations in the degree and quality of consideration given the facts. Some individuals would have read or listened to the views of authorities, sorted out irrelevancies, appraised each authority's position in light of available evidence, and weighed all possible interpretations of the facts. Others would have taken the ultimate shortcut and forgone all inquiry on the assumption that their intuition is infallible. A large middle group would have made some inquiry, but it would have been less than exhaustive and sometimes less than adequate.

Finally, we would find wide differences in the quality of judgment of the issue. Some would have judged quite objectively, avoiding preconceived notions and prejudices, and being critical of all views, including those to which they were naturally disposed. Others would have been ruled by emotion, untempered by reason, their judgment little more than a conditioned reflex. Again, most would have achieved some middle position in which thought and "gut reaction" intermingled to produce more or less objective conclusions.

□ A SAMPLE SITUATION

To see how all these differences might work in an actual moral issue, let's take the question "Is it wrong to kill enemy civilians in time of war?" Imagine that we have asked this question of a representative sampling of the general public and that a majority has answered in the negative. What variations in knowledge, inquiry, and judgment would the statistical report cover? What actual lines of thought might have occurred to the individuals in the majority? Here are some probabilities.

> Mr. A: "If they started the war, then the blame would be on them and they'd deserve no mercy. They'd all be responsible for their government's actions; so all of them, civilians and soldiers alike, would be regarded as enemies. If they get hurt, that's the breaks."
>
> Mr. B: "I fought in Vietnam and, believe me, in that war you couldn't tell a friend from an enemy. I've seen children waving and shouting greetings as they approached with explosives attached to their backs. I've seen peasants who'd shoot you in the back or direct you into a mine field after you'd given them candy. It can't be wrong to kill civilians in war because it's necessary for survival."

Ms. C: "No, it's not wrong if it helps to shorten the war. In World War II we avoided more deaths and injuries to our armed forces and brought them home sooner by dropping atom bombs on two Japanese cities. Many civilians were in those cities. But our main intention was not to kill civilians; it was to end the war. Therefore the bombing was justified."

Ms. D: "It's a complex question. It really depends on the circumstances. The bombings of Dresden, Hiroshima, and Nagasaki during World War II were very wrong in my view. Those targets were selected *because* they were population centers and their destruction would demoralize the enemy. In other words, civilians were deliberately singled out for elimination. No goal, however worthy, justifies such slaughter. On the other hand, in a guerrilla war, the distinction between combatant and noncombatant is somewhat blurred. Soldiers disguise themselves as civilians. And civilians are enlisted, sometimes against their will, to perform military acts. In such a war I can conceive of situations where the killing of civilians is justified; say, where a soldier is in doubt whether the civilian approaching him is armed and must choose to shoot or jeopardize his own life. Is it wrong to kill civilians? I'd have to say no, not necessarily."

Perhaps none of these views is the best one possible, but the last one is much more penetrating than the others. It shows a willingness to consider the differences, as well as the similarities, between particular acts of war. It reveals sensitivity to important distinctions—specifically, to the distinction between the circumstances of the World War II bombings and the conditions of a guerrilla war. Finally, it demonstrates an awareness of the dilemma faced by particular people who must make a moral decision in actual war situations, the kill-or-be-killed choice that must be made instantly, without time for careful reflection.

Although Ms. D's view is a much wiser, more informed response than the others, in a statistical report its excellence would be ignored. It would merely be lumped with the others, including the utterly shallow and morally insensitive view of Mr. A. In statistical computation, the depth or shallowness of the thought that supports the answer counts for nothing. (It is possible, of course, for statistical reports to include the full answers, but even when a report is set up to provide for such answers, which it seldom is, the need for brevity often forces their omission.)

☐ THE MAJORITY CAN ERR

In short, the majority view is less than perfect. To assume that it is necessarily enlightened is a serious mistake. If 1 percent or 49 percent of the population can be shallow or prejudiced in their view of an issue, so can 51 or 99 percent. Majority ignorance is as common as majority wisdom.

At various times in history the majority have supported outrageous deeds. In some ancient societies the majority believed in and practiced murdering female babies, abandoning crippled infants to die, murdering young men and women as sacrifices to the gods or to serve a deceased monarch in the afterlife. The majority have supported religious wars, child labor, even child prostitution. In Hitler's Germany the majority gave at least silent assent to the persecution of the Jews. For centuries the standard treatment of the mentally ill, universally accepted, bordered on torture. Until recently in the southern United States racial intermarriage was not only morally condemned but legally prohibited as well.

If the majority view determined right and wrong, then slavery was not wrong when it was practiced in America. It was right as long as the majority accepted it and became wrong only when more than 50 percent of the people rejected it. If the majority's moral perspective cannot err, then the religious persecutions that drove the early colonists to this continent were not wrong, were not vices at all, but virtues. Such a view, of course, is nonsense. Slavery and religious persecution would be no less immoral if every country in the world approved them. There must be more to right and wrong than a showing of hands.

To be sure, the majority view may be the only one a democratic society can follow in its procedures of representative government. And even in lawmaking, the majority view will rightly exert considerable influence on legislators (though an honest legislator will not hesitate to oppose the majority view when the common good is served in doing so). But even in these necessary nods to the majority, there is no guarantee of correctness. The future of the country hangs precariously on the hope that, in urgent matters, the counsel of the majority will be the counsel of wisdom.

Yet in ethical judgment, where there is a singular potential for irrational reaction, and even self-deception, it is especially important to avoid slavishly following the majority view. We do well to remember that, just as we view certain practices of past centuries as morally indefensible, later generations may judge some of our practices similarly. Every age has its blindness, perhaps even its barbarism.

⬚ SAMPLE RESPONSE

Here is a sample response to help you understand the kind of analysis and the form of response appropriate for the inquiries that follow. (You need not agree with the particular viewpoint expressed.)

Inquiry: At the beginning of the twentieth century a majority of law-makers considered it morally right to deny women the right to vote. Was the majority morally correct in this instance?

Sample Response: *The majority was wrong in this case. The lawmakers, of course, had reasons for believing women shouldn't be allowed to vote—for example, that women lacked the necessary level of intelligence and that involvement in politics would rob women of their femininity. But such reasons were not valid then and are laughable today. No* legitimate *reason ever existed for depriving women of their rights of citizenship.*

▣ INQUIRIES

If you need assistance in composing your responses, read "Writing About Moral Issues" in the Appendix.

 1. Animal rights activists continue to lobby and demonstrate to outlaw the use of animals in laboratory experiments, particularly those in which the animals suffer extreme pain. Since a majority of Americans have, at least implicitly, supported the use of animals in laboratory experiments, it might be argued that animal rights protests are unethical. Can you find anything in this chapter to support such an argument? Do you support it? Explain.

 2. Environmentalists in Oregon, by their own admission, have driven spikes into trees to prevent the lumber industry from harvesting them. If the trees are harvested, the spikes break the huge, expensive saws in the lumber mills and sometimes injure the workers. Is the use of spikes by environmentalists unethical? (Note: If your answer to this question differs from your answer to inquiry 1, justify that disagreement.)

 3. The great majority of people seem to find nothing objectionable about the use of commercials in children's television programming. Yet a distinguished panel commissioned by the National Science Foundation found reason to disagree. After reviewing twenty-one relevant scholarly studies, they concluded:

> It is clear from the available evidence that television advertising *does* influence children. Research has demonstrated that children attend to and learn from commercials, and that advertising is at least moderately

successful in creating positive attitudes toward and the desire for products advertised. The variable that emerged most clearly across numerous
studies as a strong determinant of children's perception of television
advertising is the child's age. Existing research clearly establishes that
children become more skilled in evaluating television advertising as they
grow older, and that to treat all children from 2 to 12 as a homogeneous
group masks important, perhaps crucial differences.[1]

Do you think the majority view is correct in this case? Do you think the
use of commercials in children's television programming raises any ethical questions? Explain.

4. For centuries it was the common belief among Europeans that it is
morally acceptable for society to deny Jews the rights of gentiles. That
belief resulted in the segregation of Jews in ghettos, the strict regulation
of their marriages, the imposition of special codes of dress on Jewish
women, the forced attendance at Christian religious ceremonies, and the
exclusion from certain occupations, including law, medicine, and education. Was that majority view ethically defensible?

5. After the Japanese attack on Pearl Harbor, President Roosevelt
ordered the internment of thousands of American citizens of Japanese
ancestry. (They were guilty of no crime but were considered *potentially*
disloyal because of their ancestry.) A large number of Americans, possibly
a majority, supported the president's action on moral grounds. Then,
almost half a century later, Congress awarded every Japanese American
who had been interned $20,000 in reparations. Since few people made any
public protest, a majority of the American people presumably approved
of the congressional action. Was the internment morally justified? Was the
paying of reparations?

6. The dropping of atomic bombs on Hiroshima and Nagasaki in World
War II was regarded by millions of Americans, perhaps a majority, as
a morally acceptable act. Was the dropping of those bombs morally
acceptable?

7. In 1971, a military court found Lt. William Calley guilty of the premeditated murder of twenty-two unarmed civilians in the Vietnam village of My Lai and sentenced him to dismissal from the army, forfeiture
of pay and privileges, and life imprisonment. But a national poll revealed
that 79 percent of the American public disapproved of the verdict and
punishment, presumably on moral grounds.[2] Were the verdict and punishment ethically justifiable?

8. Two years after the U.S. Supreme Court's famous school desegregation order, a national poll revealed that 80 percent of the citizens of southern states opposed school desegregation. The same poll disclosed that 76 percent disapproved of the Interstate Commerce Commission's order banning train, bus, and waiting room segregation.[3] Are such desegregation orders ethically valid?

9. At various times polls have indicated that a majority of Americans favor outlawing the Communist party. Is it ethically valid in a democracy to outlaw any political party that citizens might in good conscience choose to support?

10. A 16-year-old girl visits a birth control clinic and asks to be put on the pill. Since she is a minor, the clinic doctor who writes the prescription for her notifies her parents of the action. Possibly a majority of Americans would approve of the doctor's action. Is the action ethical?

11. In some parts of the country a majority of the citizens presumably believe that it is morally acceptable to send people to jail for smoking marijuana. Is that view correct?

12. Advancements in high technology may eliminate many jobs, particularly for the unskilled worker. The majority of labor union members believe that machines should not replace human workers. Is it ethically justifiable for a society to pursue a course of technological advancement that could leave thousands of workers without jobs?

CHAPTER THREE

THE ROLE OF FEELINGS

If the majority view does not determine the rightness of an action, should each person decide on the basis of her or his own feelings, desires, preferences?

The idea of everyone's deciding moral issues on the basis of feelings, desires, or preferences enjoys considerable popularity today. "Everyone doing her or his own thing" may seem to be a very reasonable and tolerant approach to morality. It has an understandable appeal to young people who are inclined to challenge their parents' moral code and to those of all ages who are disenchanted with traditional views. It also harmonizes well with the prevailing concern with individuality. If each person is an individual, different from all others, then each person's morality, it would seem, should, like fingerprints, reflect his or her uniqueness.

Those who take this view emphasize making one's lifestyle and moral perspective reflect one's own needs and wants rather than some prefabricated set of principles that "society" sanctions. They value subjective validity more highly than external norms.

The conclusion that follows from this reasoning is that no one person's view is preferable to another's. Each is good in its own way. One person's sacred ritual may be the next person's cardinal sin. Thus if a man and a woman want to marry, that's fine (the same for a man and a man, a woman and a woman). If a couple choose to live together without marrying, that's fine, too. Indeed, if twenty-two people want to live together in multiple liaison, that is also fine. No one other than the individuals themselves has any right to pass judgment. Freedom is the byword; rules and restrictions are the only heresies.

Let's begin by recognizing that this perspective on morality is not original. Two centuries ago French philosopher Jean Jacques Rousseau wrote, "What I feel is right is right, what I feel is wrong is wrong." The child, in Rousseau's view, is inherently good; the only corrupting influence is society with its artificial constraints. Whether or not today's champions of feelings are aware of the fact, their call to cast aside inhibitions, reject external authority, and follow one's urges is but an echo of Rousseau. That is certainly the case with the ethics education approach known as "values clarification." This system asserts that there is no universal, objective moral standard, that the only norm is what each person decides to value. The job of the educator, values clarification claims, is to encourage students to decide for themselves and then to affirm and support whatever they choose. The teacher is to be completely nonjudgmental, withholding all criticism of students' choices—the clear implication being that in the area of values *no one can ever be mistaken.*[1]

Also related to Rousseau, but more influential in modern thought than values clarification, is humanistic psychology, especially the thought of Carl Rogers. In phrasing remarkably similar to Rousseau's, Rogers assigned feelings a central role in guiding behavior: "One of the basic things which I was a long time in realizing, and which I am still learning, is that when an activity *feels* as though it is valuable or worth doing, it *is* worth doing. Put another way, I have learned that my total organismic sensing of a situation is more trustworthy than my intellect."[2] Rogers' goal in therapy was to persuade the client not only to "listen to feelings which he has always denied and repressed," including feelings that have seemed "terrible" or "abnormal" or "shameful," but also to *affirm* those feelings. Rogers was convinced that the therapist should be totally accepting of whatever the client expressed and should show "an outgoing positive feeling without reservations, without evaluations."[3]

One becomes a person, Rogers claimed, by self-affirmation rather than self-evaluation or self-criticism. The "only question that matters" for a healthy person, he maintained, is "Am I living in a way which is deeply satisfying to me, and which truly expresses me?" Pleasing others or meeting external, objective standards of behavior—such as the moral code of one's society or religion—have no role in Rogers' process.[4]

Rogers' impact on American thought, and on Western thought in general, has been profound. Together with his associate, William Coulson, Rogers developed and successfully implemented a plan to promote his value-free, nonjudgmental, nondirective approach in the teaching of both psychological counseling and ethics. (Coulson later renounced the approach, claiming that it ruined lives and harmed society.) Subsequently, two generations of psychologists, guidance counselors, student personnel staff in colleges, social workers, and even members of the clergy were trained in his method and proceeded in good faith to counsel *millions* of people to follow their feelings. The idea has been most enthusiastically embraced by the entertainment industry, which has made it a central theme of movies and television programs.

In the space of a few decades feelings have become the dominate ethical standard. As Allan Bloom concluded, "Our desire . . . is now the last word, while in the past it was the questionable and dangerous part of us." As he explains, "choice" used to mean freedom to do what one ought to do, what one determined was right to do, but "now, when we speak of the right to choice, we mean that there are no necessary consequences, that disapproval is only prejudice and guilt only a neurosis."[5]

☐ ARE FEELINGS RELIABLE?

As we noted in Chapter 2, there is no magic in majorities, so the fact that millions of people have adopted Rogers' implicit faith in feelings, desires, and preferences does not prove that such faith is warranted. Can feelings be trusted to guide human behavior? No reasonable person would deny that *some* feelings, desires, and preferences are admirable and therefore make excellent guides. Albert Schweitzer's feeling of "reverence for life" led him to choose the life of a medical missionary in then-primitive Africa over artistic and scholarly pursuits in Europe. Martin Luther King, Jr.'s passion for justice led him to heroic leadership in the civil rights movement. Mother Teresa's compassion for the world's poor and suffering inspired a life of self-sacrificing service to others. And countless caring people the world over, who never become well-known, are moved by love of neighbor to make the world a little better. Oseola McCarty is a good example. Forced to go to work in 1919 at age 11, she washed and ironed clothes for a living all her life, always putting as much money as she could afford in the bank. Then at age 87 she donated almost the entire amount—$150,000—to set up a college scholarship fund for deserving young people in her hometown.[6]

Honesty, however, demands acknowledgment of the darker aspect of feelings. When Hitler exterminated more than 6 million Jews and Stalin massacred 30 million Russian peasants, they were following their feelings, as was their common spiritual ancestor, Genghis Khan, when he led his hordes of Mongols across Asia and into Europe, plundering, raping, and devastating. Serial killer Ted Bundy murdered young women and Jeffrey Dahmer practiced cannibalism for no other reason than to satisfy their desires. And for that same reason a group of Nassau County, New York, men used gifts to lure boys—some as young as 7, most of them fatherless—into homosexual seduction and then threatened them with beatings and even death if they told the authorities.[7]

If Rousseau and Rogers are correct in claiming that everything is a matter of personal preference and whatever feels good is good, then the concept of moral excellence is meaningless and Hitler, Stalin, Bundy, and Dahmer deserve to be considered *the moral equals* of Schweitzer, King, and Mother Teresa. Furthermore, if Rousseau and Rogers are correct, there is no ethical basis for condemning genocide, murder, cannibalism, and child molestation. And without an ethical basis, the laws forbidding these deeds are no longer valid and the people that have been imprisoned for committing them should be released. Logic is uncompromising in such matters and does not allow the luxury of ignoring the implications of ideas. Rather, it demands that we evaluate ideas by their implications. In this case, that means judging Rousseau's and Rogers' idea to be unreasonable.

□ A Better Guide Is Needed

When we are thinking clearly and being honest with ourselves, we realize that there is a potential in each of us for noble actions of high purpose and honor; but there is also a potential for great mischief and wickedness. Each of us is capable of a wide range of deeds, some that would make us proud if the whole world knew, and others that, if discovered by a single other person, would cause us shame.

A man passing a department store late at night may have a sudden urge to smash the window and steal the cashmere sports jacket he lusts after. A student may feel like spreading a lie about her roommate to avenge a real or imagined wrong. A bank employee may have the desire and even a plan to embezzle a million dollars and depart for the South Seas. Any one of us, however placid our nature, may on occasion experience an overwhelming urge to punch someone in the nose. Yet each of these actions is at least of questionable rightness, *despite* the feelings and desires of the person involved.

Similarly, a person walking alone on the shore of a lake may prefer to ignore the call for help that comes from the water. A surgeon relaxing at home may prefer not to answer the call to perform emergency surgery. The father who promised to take his children on a picnic may prefer to play golf with his friends. A lawyer may prefer not to spend the necessary time preparing for the defense of her client. In such situations the answer "whatever the person prefers to do is right to do" is hollow. Good sense suggests that the right action may be at odds with the individual's preference.

Ironically, morality by feelings *completely ignores other people's feelings.* Those who are acted against surely have feelings, too; in the cases cited above their feelings presumably run counter to the feelings of those committing the actions. If the murder victims had been consulted, they surely would have expressed a preference not to be so treated. Similarly, few people enjoy being robbed, lied about, assaulted, or neglected in their time of need. To say that we should be free to do as we wish without regard for others is to say that others should be free to do as they wish without regard for us.* If such a rule were followed, the result would be social chaos.

Since our feelings, desires, and preferences can be either beneficial or harmful, noble or ignoble, praiseworthy or damnable, and since they can be either in harmony or in conflict with other people's feelings, desires, and preferences, they are obviously not accurate criteria for analysis of moral issues or trustworthy guidelines to action. Feelings, desires, and preferences need to be evaluated and judged. They need to be measured against some *impartial* standard that will reveal their quality. To make them the basis of our moral decisions is to ignore those needs and to accept them uncritically as the measure of their own worth.

▦ SAMPLE RESPONSE

Here is a sample response to help you understand the kind of analysis and the form of response appropriate for the inquiries that follow. (You need not agree with the particular viewpoint expressed.) Note that the response expresses not just the writer's moral judgment but also the reasoning that underlies it.

Inquiry: Marian is a 55-year-old widow whose children no longer live at home. Lonely and bored, Marian has sought escape in alcohol. Each

---

*The argument that people may do whatever they desire to do "as long as no one else is hurt" may seem related, but it is really quite different. It has a social dimension (consideration for others) in addition to a personal dimension (what one wants to do). Unfortunately, it begs the question of whether we have a right to injure *ourselves.*

night after work, she drinks four or five highballs, sometimes followed by a couple of glasses of wine with dinner. (Not infrequently, she falls asleep on the couch and misses dinner.) When a well-meaning neighbor commented on her drinking, Marian replied, "I feel that if I get up and go to work every day and don't harm anyone, there's nothing wrong with my having a drink at night." Is her feeling reasonable?

Sample Response: *To begin with, five highballs followed by a couple of glasses of wine is considerably more than "a drink." In addition, when she says she's not hurting anyone, she's forgetting at least one person—herself. Using alcohol to cope with life is emotionally harmful, and consuming that much alcohol is physically harmful. It is also difficult to imagine that she performs her work well. Far from guiding her well, Marian's feelings are victimizing her. The moral thing for Marian to do, in my judgment, is to quit fooling herself and get help for her drinking problem.*

▨ INQUIRIES

If you need assistance in composing your responses, read "Writing About Moral Issues" in the Appendix.

1. Ada Dupree died at age 104 and her family intended to bury her in the North Florida town where she had lived all her life and was the oldest citizen—and where she had been a caring friend to whites and blacks alike. That had been her final wish. But then came threats from angry white people to shoot at her hearse and her mourners if the burial were held in the town's white cemetery. So she was buried in a black cemetery in a neighboring town. The feelings that made those white people oppose Ada Dupree's burial in the local cemetery were evidently powerful and deeply held. Were they also morally right? (It should be noted that not all white people in the town had these feelings. One white woman offered to give her own burial plot for Dupree. And others attended the funeral.)[8]

2. Clark lives in a state that has a 7 percent sales tax on automobiles. Even when a person buys a used car from the owner, he or she must file a form with the motor vehicle department, stating the purchase price and paying the appropriate amount of tax. Clark has found the car he wants. The price of $4000 is within his means, but he doesn't feel that he should have to pay the additional $280 in tax. So he tells the seller, "I'll pay you

$4000 for the car if you give me a sales receipt for $1200. That way I'll only have to pay $94." The seller shares Clark's feeling about paying the tax, so he agrees. Is their action morally wrong? Explain.

3. Morey is a sadist. In other words, he enjoys causing other people pain. The feelings he experiences when he hurts others are exciting and deeply satisfying. Do these feelings justify the actions that produce them? Why or why not?

4. A Little League baseball coach anticipates a poor season because he lacks a competent pitcher. Just before the season begins, a new family moves into his neighborhood. The coach discovers that one of the boys in the family is an excellent pitcher, but that he is over the age limit for Little League participation. Because the family is not known in the area, the coach is sure he can use the boy without being discovered. He wants a winning season very much, for himself and for his team. Is he morally justified in using the boy?

5. Ralph, a college student, borrows his roommate's car to drive to his aunt's funeral. On the way back he falls asleep at the wheel, veers off the road, and rolls down an embankment. Though he emerges unhurt, the car is a total wreck. Since the car is five years old, the roommate has no collision insurance. Ralph is sorry about the accident but feels no responsibility for paying his roommate what the car was worth. Does he have any moral responsibility to do so?

6. The owner of a roadside restaurant prefers not to serve black or Hispanic customers. She paid for the property, she reasons, and has spent many years developing the business; therefore, she should have the right to decide whom she serves. Is her white-only preference ethically defensible?

7. A small city has a zoning ordinance. The spirit of that ordinance clearly prohibits the operating of a business in areas designated "residential." However, the wording is such that a loophole exists. One woman wishes to open a pet shop in the basement of her split-level home. The law is in her favor. Is morality?

8. The executives of three large appliance companies get together to discuss their competitive situation. Among them they account for 91 percent of the U.S. production of their particular products. They decide that by stabilizing their prices, they can benefit their stockholders, invest more money in product research, and thereby deliver a better product to the consumer. They agree to consult one another before setting prices and to price comparable models at the same price. Is this action ethically acceptable?

9. A man buys a house and later realizes he has paid too much money for it. In fact, he has been badly cheated. There is a bad leak in the cellar and through one wall, the furnace is not functioning properly, and the well is dry at certain times during the year. The cost of putting these things right will be prohibitive. He wants to "unload" the house as soon as possible, and he prefers to increase his chances of recovering his investment by concealing the truth about the house's condition. Is it right for him to do so?

10. For over half a century a funeral home in Charlotte, North Carolina, displayed an embalmed human body in a glass showcase. The body was that of a carnival worker who was killed in a fight in 1911. The man's father, also a carnival worker, paid part of the funeral costs and asked the funeral home director to keep the body until he returned. Nothing more was heard from him. Thus the body, clad only in a loincloth, remained on display for sixty-one years. Public clamor finally resulted in its removal from public view. However, the funeral home director (the son of the original director) allegedly felt nothing was wrong in exhibiting the body, which he compared to a mummy in a museum.[9] Is his feeling ethically sound?

11. A newspaper columnist signs a contract with a newspaper chain. Several months later she is offered a position with another newspaper chain at a higher salary. Because she would prefer making more money, she notifies the first chain that she is breaking her contract. The courts will decide the legality of her action. But what of the morality? Did the columnist behave ethically?

12. A California businessman started a check-cashing service, operating out of a large commercial van. He charges customers 1 1/2 percent of the face value of the check for the service, and he has plenty of customers, mainly people on unemployment, welfare, social security, and disability, who lack the bank accounts and credit ratings necessary to cash their checks in a bank. His profit is estimated at almost $50,000 per year. He feels there is nothing unethical about his business.[10] Do you agree?

13. In Mineola, New York, a police officer allegedly posed as a clinical psychologist during his off-duty hours and made phone calls to numerous women inquiring about their sex lives.[11] Presumably he felt that his desire to adopt the pose and make the calls was sufficient to justify his doing so. Do you agree with him?

14. A 16-year-old girl and her father were arrested in Panama City, Florida, for allegedly trying to sell the girl's unborn baby for a ten-year-old car and $500.[12] Although selling babies is against the law, the two presumably felt that they had the moral right to do so. Is their feeling morally defensible?

15. Two workers were displaced when a company installed a robot to deliver tools and materials to workers in the plant. The robot followed a specially painted track on the plant floor. Several other workers, fearing that their jobs would also be lost, decided to "teach the company a lesson." They repainted the track so that the robot walked off the loading dock and suffered major damage. The workers felt they were justified in their action. Is this an ethically defensible position?

16. An office worker had a record of frequent absence. He used all his vacation and sick leave days and frequently requested additional leave without pay. His supervisor and coworkers expressed great frustration because his absenteeism caused bottlenecks in paperwork, created low morale in the office, and required others to do his work in addition to their own. On the other hand, he felt he was entitled to take his earned time and additional time off without pay. Was he right?

CHAPTER FOUR

THE ROLE OF CONSCIENCE

*If feelings are no better a guide than the majority
view, is the basis of morality each person's own
conscience? How trustworthy is conscience?*

The term *conscience* is so common and often so carelessly used, that for
many people it has little meaning. Precisely what is a conscience? Does
everybody have one or are some people born without one? Are all consciences "created equal"? Are our consciences influenced by the attitudes
and values of our culture? Can we do anything to develop our consciences, or are they fixed and unchangeable? These important issues
must be considered before we can decide whether conscience is a reliable
moral guide.

Over the centuries philosophers have disagreed in their definitions of
conscience. Some have defined it as the voice of God speaking directly to
the individual soul. The problem with this definition is that in cases
where conscience does not inform a person that an act is wrong (or mis-
informs the person), the implication is that God has failed that person.
Such an idea is unacceptable to religious people. Others have defined conscience as a mirror of custom, a mere reflection of what our culture has
taught us. This definition also creates a problem: It leaves unexplained
those cases in which conscience directs us to *defy* custom.

Still others have argued that conscience is a special sense, a moral
sense, that is innate in human beings. This may come closest to being a
workable definition, but it also poses difficulties that must not be overlooked. The term *sense* usually suggests an essentially developed faculty

associated with a particular organ—the sense of sight, with the eyes; the sense of hearing, with the ears; and so on. Conscience cannot be *that kind* of sense. When we say, "My conscience is bothering me" or "My conscience is clear," we are not talking of any *physical* condition.

What kind of sense can conscience be? It is the kind that depends upon the nurturing it receives over the years to realize its potential, the kind that must be trained to be trustworthy. Although no comparison can be completely accurate, we might compare conscience to our sense of appreciation of beauty. Like conscience, this sense is present in everyone, is not a physical phenomenon, is subject to a variety of influences, and depends for its highest realization on conscious development.

The reason physical terms are inadequate to explain conscience is that it is not a physical but a metaphysical reality. Thus, we can describe what it *does* much better than what it *is*. The same situation exists with the metaphysical reality we call *intellect*. We perceive that our intellects serve to apprehend truth and distinguish it from error and to apprehend beauty and distinguish it from ugliness. Similarly, we perceive that our consciences serve to apprehend good and distinguish it from evil.

□ INDIVIDUAL DIFFERENCES

Simple observation will demonstrate that the intensity of conscience differs from person to person. Even as small children most of us have perceived, however vaguely, that our playmates and relatives appear to differ widely in this phenomenon. Preschoolers will often grab toys away from others. Some of them will never show (and if externals are a mirror to internal states of mind, never *feel*) the slightest remorse. Yet others will be so aware of the offensiveness of such behavior that they will immediately be saddened and repentant; their remorse will be evident. Hours later they will still be trying to make amends.

The classmates of a grade school stutterer will vary greatly in their attitude toward him. Many will treat him as a nonperson, an object to tease and taunt and mimic. Some will simply know no better and will be unaware that their actions are wrong. Others will at some moment sense that they have caused him pain and will feel ashamed of their behavior.

Such differences in conscience are observable in adults as well. Some people are very sensitive to the effects of their actions, acutely aware when they have done wrong. Others are relatively insensitive, unconscious of their offenses, free from feelings of remorse. They live their lives uninterested in self-examination or self-criticism, seldom even considering whether something *should* be done. Others see right and wrong as applying to only a limited number of matters—sexual behavior, for example, and deportment within the family. The affairs of citizenship and business or professional conduct are, to them, outside the sphere of morality. Still others were at one time morally sensitive, but have succeeded in neutralizing the promptings of conscience with elaborate rationalizations. When Claude's wife expresses disapproval of his cramming the hotel's soap and towels and rugs and bedspreads into his suitcase, he says, "Look, the hotels in this country expect you to take a few souvenirs. They build the cost into their room rates. If I take a bit more than they've allowed for, they write it off on their tax returns."

Finally, there are the extremists: the scrupulous and the lax. Scrupulous people are morally sensitive beyond reasonableness, often to the point of compulsion. They see moral faults where there are none. Every action, however trivial—whether to peel the potatoes or cook them whole, whether to polish the car today or tomorrow—is an excruciating moral dilemma. Their counterparts at the other pole are virtually without conscience, using other people as things, unmindful of their status as persons, pursuing only what satisfies the almighty *me*.

□ THE SHAPERS OF CONSCIENCE

Many people have the vague notion that their consciences are solely a product of their own intellectual efforts, without outside influence. They imagine themselves having devoted a period of time, precisely *when* they are not sure, perhaps during their teenage years, to carefully evaluating various ideas of right and wrong and then forming their own moral perspective. That this notion should exist is understandable. People are naturally more aware of their conscious mental life than of any outside influences, particularly subtle ones. In addition, the thought that one's life is and has always been completely under one's control is very reassuring. In any case, *the notion is wrong.*

Conscience is shaped by two forces that are essentially outside our control—natural endowment and social conditioning—and one that is, in some measure, within our control—moral choice. The specific attributes of our conscience, including its sensitivity to moral issues and the degree of its influence on our behavior, are attributable to one or more of these forces. Let's examine each force in turn.

NATURAL ENDOWMENT

A person's basic temperament and level and kind of intelligence are largely "in the genes." Both temperament and intelligence play a considerable role in shaping the total personality. The person with a practical intelligence and the person with a philosophic intelligence will not have the same potential for ethical analysis or the same potential for perceptiveness in moral issues. This is not to say that the two kinds of intelligence are mutually exclusive. Some people, happily, have both. There are, after all, philosophers of science and philosophers of technology; and the contributions of mathematicians to modern philosophy have been considerable. Neither is it to say that those with more philosophical potential always use that potential, or that this factor is always so dominant as to make them have more developed consciences. It is to say that the kind of intelligence one has, like the degree of intelligence, opens some doors of potentiality and closes others. Similarly, the basic temperament, largely a matter of one's metabolism, poses certain obstacles and opportunities in the development of conscience.

For example, the vivacious, energetic person, quick of movement and speech, who constantly performs in metabolic overdrive, may tend to be somewhat less disposed to careful analysis of past actions than is the slower, more reflective person. The impulsive person, impatient to do and have done, may be virtually incapable of prior reflection. Conscience, in this case, may operate only after the fact. It is not, of course, a matter of one disposition, one metabolic rate, being preferable to another. Each presents some fertile areas for the development and use of conscience, and each presents some barren ones.

SOCIAL CONDITIONING

Conditioning is the most neglected shaper of conscience. Yet, ironically, it is in many ways the most important. Conditioning may be defined as the myriad effects of our environment: the people, places, institutions, ideas, and values we are exposed to as we grow and develop. We are conditioned first by our early social and religious training from parents. This influence may be partly conscious and partly unconscious on their part, and indirect as well as direct. It is so pervasive that all our later attitudes—political, economic, sociological, psychological, theological—in some way bear its imprint.

If children are brought up in an ethnocentric environment—that is, one in which the group (race, nationality, culture, or special value system) believes it is superior to others—research shows that they will tend to be less tolerant than other people. More specifically they will tend to make hard right-wrong, good-bad classifications. If they cannot identify with a group, they must oppose it. In addition, they will tend to need an "out group," some outsiders whom they can blame for real and imagined wrongs. This in turn makes it difficult or impossible for them to identify with humanity as a whole or to achieve undistorted understanding of others.[1]

In addition, ethnocentric people, even as children, show an inability to deal with complex situations. As a result, such people learn to see and think about their daily transactions with other people and ideas in an oversimplified manner. Their way of thinking demands simple solutions to problems, even to problems that do not admit of simple solutions.[2]

The influence of such training on conscience is obvious. Although few of us are subjected to a purely ethnocentric environment as children, elements of it are common in most environments in one way or another. The effects on us, though less dramatic and pronounced, are nevertheless real and a significant shaping force on our conscience.

We are also conditioned by our encounters with brothers, sisters, relatives, friends. We see a sister's observance or disregard of family rules or her habit of lying to parents. An uncle brings a present he has stolen from work. Our playmates cheat in games. More important, we see not only these actions, but the reactions of the people themselves and of others who observe them. We are witness to all the moral contradictions, all the petty hypocrisies of those around us. We ourselves act—now in observance of some parental rule, then against another—and we sense pleasure or pain. We imitate others' strategies for justifying questionable behavior.

Next we are conditioned by our experiences in grade school, by our widening circle of acquaintances, and perhaps by our beginning contact with institutional religion. We perceive similarities and differences in the attitudes of our teachers and classmates. We observe their behavior, form impressions, sense (quite subliminally and vaguely, to be sure) the level and development of their consciences. We meet and learn from our priest, minister, or rabbi. Perhaps in all these situations it is not the formal so much as the informal contact, the mere introduction to their personalities, habits, patterns of behavior, that affects us in dramatic, though subconscious, ways. Though memory may cloud, experience remains indelible.

We are then conditioned by our contact with people, places, and ideas through books, radios, newspapers, magazines, tapes and CDs, and especially television programming. What we see and hear makes an impact on our attitudes and values, sometimes blatantly, sometimes subtly. Situation comedies instruct us as to what may appropriately be laughed at and/or ridiculed. Soap operas and dramatic programs train our emotions to respond favorably or unfavorably to different behaviors. Talk shows inform us of what celebrities think about a variety of subjects, including right and wrong. And commercials incessantly tell us what possessions and living styles will make us happy and are therefore desirable. As the entertainment and communications media have grown more numerous and more sophisticated, the number of individuals and groups involved in social conditioning has multiplied, and their messages are often at odds with those of home and church and school.

MORAL CHOICE

Long before we were able to make authentic moral choices, heredity and social conditioning had already shaped our conscience, and they continued the process even when, as small children, we made rudimentary choices. Children's choices, after all, are not fully *conscious* acts but mere assertions of will that express their inherited traits or imitation of others' behavior. A toddler's obeying or defying her parents' directions is an example of such choosing. Only in later childhood do we develop the ability to weigh alternatives and make *reasoned* moral choices. The problem is that by then we will have already developed attitudes and patterns of response to situations and people, at least some of which are likely to be morally undesirable and difficult to change.

That people tend to behave in ways that are consistent with their thinking is fairly well known. What is not so well known is that the reverse also occurs—they think in ways that justify their behavior. The eminent English scholar, Dr. Samuel Johnson, explained the two tendencies as follows:

> Not only [do] our speculations influence our practice, but our practice reciprocally influences our speculations. We not only do what we approve, but there is danger lest in time we come to approve what we do . . . for no other reason than that we do it. A man is always desirous of being at peace with himself; and when he cannot reconcile his passions to [his] conscience, he will attempt to reconcile his conscience to his passions.[3]

Note the word "passions," a synonym for the term that is causing so much moral confusion today—"feelings." Dr. Johnson knew what was pointed out in the previous chapter, that feelings are not a reliable guide in moral matters. Furthermore, as he implies here, when feelings are allowed to overrule conscience, conscience loses its moral bearings. It becomes desire's puppet, telling us what we *want* to hear instead of what

we *need* to hear. One doesn't have to be morally disreputable to be victimized by this process. It can ensnare respectable, well-intentioned people who not only want to make wise moral choices but *honestly believe they
are doing so,* as the following examples illustrate:

> A police detective was investigating a rape case, in which the victim had
> recorded part of the perpetrator's license number. The detective eventu-
> ally found a suspect who matched the description of a rapist in almost
> every way. There was only one problem—his license plate number did
> not match. Rather than lose the case on what seemed a technicality, the
> detective changed the victim's statement, inserting the suspect's plate
> number. The detective did not consider this action immoral; he believed
> he was just bolstering his case, even though his action effectively elimi-
> nated exoneration based on "reasonable doubt."[4]

> A number of newspapers around the country have a policy of
> including the cause of death in every obituary, even if the family of the
> deceased asks that it be omitted. (For example, the obituary might state
> that the cause of death was suicide by suffocation, slashed wrists, or a
> gunshot wound to the head.) The editorial staffs that make this policy
> apparently do so with a clear conscience, despite the fact that many
> grieving families suffer embarrassment and shame as a result.

> When actor Hugh Grant was arrested for consorting with a prosti-
> tute in Los Angeles, Grant's friend, Academy Award–winning actress
> Emma Thompson, described her reaction in an interview: "I thought,
> thank God, you know, you've broken out." She reportedly went on to say
> that what Grant had done was not something to be ashamed of but
> "wonderful, absolutely wonderful."[5] Evidently, from her moral perspec-
> tive, Grant's unfaithfulness to his fiancée and possible exposure to sexu-
> ally transmitted disease, including AIDS, not only posed no moral issue
> but were in some unspecified way *admirable!*

□ A BALANCED VIEW OF CONSCIENCE

The unpleasant realities we have noted about conscience demonstrate
that it is not an infallible moral guide. However, to leap from that evidence to the conclusion that conscience is without value would be a mistake. For all its imperfections, conscience is the most important single
guide to right and wrong an individual can have. It is, as the saying goes,
the "proximate norm of morality." For this reason, when circumstances
demand an immediate moral choice, we should follow our conscience.
(The only alternative would be to violate it, to choose to do what at that

moment seems immoral.) However, whenever circumstances allow us time to reflect on the choice conscience recommends, we should use that time to analyze the issue critically and to consider the possibility that a different choice might be better.

In short, we should follow our conscience, but not blindly. True freedom, true individuality, and real moral growth lie in examining conscience, evaluating its promptings, purging it of negative influences and error, and reinforcing it with searching ethical inquiry and penetrating ethical judgment. The chapters that follow contain helpful criteria for further developing your conscience.

Accordingly, for our purposes in examining moral issues in this and subsequent chapters, the answer "It's a matter for the individual's conscience to decide" will be inappropriate. Let's consider a few cases to see exactly why. A high school girl hears a rumor that a classmate is a shoplifter. Is she morally justified in repeating the story to her best friend if she makes the friend promise not to "tell a soul"? A 13-year-old boy walks into his neighborhood grocery store and asks the grocer for a pack of cigarettes "for my mother." The grocer knows the mother doesn't smoke and that the boy is too young to buy cigarettes legally. Should she sell them to him? A weapons manufacturer has an opportunity to make a big and very profitable sale to the ruler of a small foreign country. He knows the ruler is a tyrant who oppresses his people and governs by terror. Is it right for him to sell the weapons? A college student's friends are all sleeping with their boyfriends and are urging her to "loosen up" and follow their example. (Her boyfriend is not opposed to the idea.) She can't decide, and the more she ponders the matter, the more confused she gets. What should she do?

Whatever we decide is right in these cases, our decision should be based on more than saying "leave the matter to the individual's conscience." If we say that in the first three cases, we are saying, in effect, "Any action is acceptable," for we can have no way of knowing exactly what those people's consciences will prompt them to do. If we say it in the case of the college student, we are evading the issue, for her dilemma is deciding whether the promptings of her conscience are reasonable.

⊞ SAMPLE RESPONSE

Here is a sample response to help you understand the kind of analysis and the form of response appropriate for the inquiries that follow. (You need not agree with the particular viewpoint expressed.) Note that the response expresses not just the writer's moral judgment but also the reasoning that underlies it.

Inquiry: A graduate school professor has several student assistants, talented young men and women pursuing doctorates. He regularly uses their research findings and interpretations, and even their phrasing, in his own scholarly writing, without crediting them either in the text of his articles and books or in the footnotes. "It's part of their job to do research for me," he reasons; "the money they receive from their fellowships for doing the research is credit enough for them. " His conscience does not trouble him. But should it?

Sample Response: *His conscience should trouble him because what he is doing is unethical and the argument he offers to support his actions is flawed. Book publishers don't put someone else's name on an author's book on the grounds that the royalties he'll earn will be "credit enough." A person's ideas and the words used to express them are possessions. It doesn't matter whether the person in question is a famous scholar or a student. Taking ideas without permission is no different from stealing the computer that recorded them. There's also the element of deception to be considered. The professor is tricking members of his profession into giving him recognition and honor that he doesn't deserve.*

▣ INQUIRIES

If you need assistance in composing your responses, read "Writing About Moral Issues" in the Appendix.

1. A number of medical centers around the United States now offer "finders' fees" to physicians for referring patients to researchers who are conducting trials of new drug therapies, the side effects of which are not yet known. One researcher, for example, was offering physicians a $350 payment for each referred patient who enrolled in the research project. Many physicians accept the fees and make the referrals, apparently without suffering pangs of conscience. Are their actions ethical?[6]

2. From 1940 to 1970 more than 4,000 radiation experiments were performed on tens of thousands of Americans, many of them poor and uneducated, without their informed consent. Examples of alleged incidents:

children in a Massachusetts orphanage were fed radioisotopes; 829 pregnant Tennessee women were fed radioactive iron; patients in Rochester, New York, were injected with plutonium; cancer patients in Cincinnati received heavy doses of gamma rays. Not all of these experiments can be attributed to researchers' ignorance of the harmful effects of radiation; the main purpose of the studies was to identify those effects rather than to cure the patients. Even so, the researchers do not seem to have thought they were committing a moral offense. Were they?[7]

3. Marvin manufactures locks and keys for automobiles, and his biggest customers are General Motors, Chrysler, and Ford. But he also has a mail-order business, in which he offers (among other products) master keys for automobile locks. He realizes that his mail-order customers include more than a few car thieves, but that does not trouble his conscience. He reasons that he is not responsible for the illegal ways his products might be used. Is he correct?

4. When Bruno and Bertha rented their apartment, they signed a lease that included a provision that animals were not allowed. Now they have decided they want to have a cat. They plan to sneak it into the apartment at night so the landlord won't know they have it. Comment.

5. Lucille owns a telephone answering service. In order to check on the courtesy and helpfulness of her telephone operators, she often monitors incoming business calls. Though others might consider this to be spying, she believes it is part of her responsibility to her customers. Is it?

6. Sylvester is the descendant of a nineteenth-century "robber baron." (A robber baron is an unscrupulous individual who gains wealth by unethical means, such as by paying off legislators, exploiting employees, or savaging the environment.) Though embarrassed by the way his family's wealth was acquired, Sylvester nevertheless believes he is entitled to keep it because he inherited it. Is he correct?

7. For each of the following cases, decide whether the person's conscience was correct. That is, decide whether the action it directed her or him to take (or silently approved) is ethically justifiable. Explain your reasoning.

a. Broderick stops at a pay phone to make a call. As he is talking, he absentmindedly fingers the coin return and finds a dime someone has carelessly forgotten. When he is finished talking, he pockets the coin and walks away. Halfway down the block, he feels guilty for taking it. He returns to the booth and deposits it in the coin return.

b.   A doctor is driving down the highway late at night. She sees a car in the opposite lane swerve sharply off the road and plunge down an embankment. No other cars are around. Her first impulse as a physician is to stop and assist the victims. However, she remembers that the state has no "Good Samaritan law" to protect her from a malpractice lawsuit. Her conscience tells her she is justified in driving on.

c.   A candidate for the local school board has heard the rumor that her opponent gives "wild parties." As she proceeds with her campaign, she visits the homes of many voters. She makes it a point to tell everyone what she has heard about her opponent, always adding, "Of course, it's only a rumor that no one has yet proven to be true." She believes sincerely that it would be dishonest of her not to inform them about the rumor, so that they can evaluate it before voting.

d.   In order to beat out the competition for a summer gardener's job at a nearby estate, Alan agreed to work for a wage somewhat lower than the standard of the area. The owner and her family are at the estate only on weekends and Alan works alone. Although his workday is fixed—9 to 5, Monday through Friday—he arrives late and leaves early on most days and occasionally takes an afternoon off. He does not feel guilty because his employer is paying him less than others would have worked for.

e.   An enterprising black real estate broker hires a white man and woman to buy a house in a white neighborhood and then transfer title to her. She then visits the white residents of the neighborhood and explains that she owns one house already and plans to buy others and sell them to black families. She tells each white resident that some other white neighbor has secretly agreed to sell. Everyone becomes frightened that property values will plummet, and many are tricked into selling to the broker at much lower prices than their homes are worth. The broker then sells the homes to black families for what they are really worth. Not only does she feel morally blameless, but she regards herself as a heroine of sorts, a fighter against discrimination in housing.

f.   Fred is the oldest of seven children of a widow. He is an honor student in a technical program at a nearby junior college. He pays his way by stealing automobile tires, radios, and stereo tape decks and selling them. When he first took up this part-time "occupation," he felt a little guilty. But he no longer does, for he decided that no one is really injured: The owners will be somewhat inconvenienced but not deprived because their insurance will cover replacement costs.

8. The following people all have clear consciences. Decide whether they are entitled to them and explain your decision.

    a. George believes strongly that drug use and dealing are a personal matter, outside the sphere of morality. He sells marijuana, cocaine, heroin, anything. Whatever there is a market for, he will deal in.

    b. Gus specializes in LSD, which he laces liberally with strychnine to increase his profits.

    c. Mary Jane sells marijuana.

    d. Connie believes strongly that the use of any drug is a crutch and that hard drugs ruin lives. She volunteers to be an undercover agent at her college, without pay.

9. The consciences of the people in the following cases are confused. As a result, the people cannot decide whether the actions they are contemplating are morally right. Decide for them and present the rationale for your position.

    a. A married couple discover that their 22-year-old daughter, a college senior, is a lesbian. They are shocked and dismayed, for they regard this as moral degeneracy. They are thinking of refusing to attend her graduation and refusing to welcome her in their home until she renounces this sexual preference.

    b. A student is taking a composition course in college. Her assignment is to write on the morality of war. Back in her room she moans aloud that she doesn't know where to begin with such a complex subject. One of her roommates declares where she stands on the issue. The other challenges her view. In time, several students wander into the room and get involved in the ensuing discussion. One goes out and gets a term paper she did on a similar subject. She reads it aloud and is interrupted from time to time as someone disputes a statement or expands upon it. After an hour or so, the session breaks up, leaving the student who didn't know where to begin with a different problem: deciding to what extent, if any, she is justified in using in her paper the facts and opinions she heard from the others.

c. Harry has been an officer in the police department of his small city for a year. He has seen many violations of department policy: squad car teams pulling over on lonely streets and sleeping during evening shifts, officers receiving "quiet money" from gamblers and dope pushers, officers conducting sexual commerce with women in the station house while on duty, sergeants and lieutenants spending whole shifts at home and altering duty records to cover their absences. Harry is seriously considering turning these men in, but he is confused about where his loyalty should lie.

d. An airline pilot goes for his regular medical checkup. The doctor discovers that he has developed a heart murmur. The pilot has only a month to go before he is eligible for retirement. The doctor knows this, and wonders whether, under these unusual circumstances, she is justified in withholding the information about the pilot's condition.

10. Animal lovers in a suburb of Los Angeles picketed a parochial school to protest the action of a priest-educator. The priest had drowned ten cats because they were too noisy and messy. He explained that his action had been "humane" and added, "I buried them. They're fertilizing our rose bushes."[8] Apparently, the priest's conscience didn't bother him. Should it have?

11. A cosmetologist in a local beauty salon enjoys a high sales record and popularity with his clients. He believes that being attractive is extremely important and that his job is to help his clients feel that they are or could be attractive. Although he realizes that some of his compliments are false and that some of the products he sells do not live up to advertising claims, he feels he is performing a public service by making people feel good about themselves.

CHAPTER FIVE

COMPARING CULTURES

If an action that is praised in one culture may be condemned in another, would it be correct to say that all moral values are relative to the culture they are found in? Isn't it a mark of ignorance to pass judgments on other cultures or to claim that one culture is better than another?

Before continuing our search for a dependable standard of ethical judgment, it will be useful to consider the issue of whether moral judgments are ever appropriate outside one's own culture. Early anthropological studies of Eskimo, Samoan, and other (from the Western perspective) "exotic" cultures generated considerable debate of this issue. As the twentieth century progressed, cross-cultural communication improved and knowledge of other cultures expanded, and the focus of anthropologists' curiosity shifted from "exotic" foreign cultures to the many subcultures within their own country. In the United States, the list of subcultures would include African American, Irish American, Italian American, and Asian American. Narrower divisions according to religion, socioeconomic level, geography, gender, and sexual orientation are all possible. Thus a researcher might examine the attitudes and values of white female "yuppies" (Young Urban Professionals) living in the southeastern United States.

Contemporary scholarly discussion of cultures and subcultures is significantly affected by the social movement known as *multiculturism.* Among the central tenets of this movement are that every race or ethnic group has its own values and characteristic behaviors, that no group's values are any better or worse than any other's, and that criticism of another culture's ideas and actions is wrong. Our concern in this chapter

43

is not with multiculturalism itself, but only with its influence on ethics. We'll begin our analysis by considering differences in ethical standards among cultures.

□ DIFFERENCES AMONG CULTURES

Cultures differ in their ideas about right and wrong, and the differences are not always slight. In some instances, one culture's sin is another's virtue. For example, the conception of marriage that Americans are most familiar with—one wife and one husband joined for life—is not universal. In some cultures serial monogamy—marrying several times—is not merely tolerated (as it is beginning to be in the United States), but is regarded as neutral or even good. And in Siberia, "a Koryak woman . . . would find it hard to understand how a woman could be so selfish and so undesirous of female companionship in the home as to wish to restrict her husband to one mate."[1]

Sex before marriage has been generally viewed as immoral in the West. Yet in some island cultures, it is encouraged. Homosexuals are hounded and tormented as immoral deviants in some cultures; in others they are accepted without reservation.

Such differences are not limited to sexual morality. It is considered a person's moral obligation in some cultures to assist a blood relative in any enterprise, even stealing from others. Certain tribes of headhunters may raid neighboring villages and return with the villagers' heads for no other reason than that their "supply" of names has been used up and before a new name may be claimed, one must possess the head it belonged to.[2]

It is commonly thought that at least one action—the taking of life— would be unanimously condemned by people of all cultures. Here is what anthropologist Ruth Benedict has to say about that idea in her classic study, *Patterns of Culture:*

> On the contrary, in a matter of homicide, it may be held that one is blameless if diplomatic relations have been severed between neighboring countries, or that one kills by custom his first two children, or that a husband has right of life and death over his wife, or that it is the duty of the child to kill his parents before they are old. It may be that those are killed who steal a fowl, or who cut their upper teeth first, or who are born on a Wednesday. Among some peoples a person suffers torments at having caused an accidental death; among others it is a matter of no consequence. Suicide also may be a light matter, the recourse of anyone who has suffered some slight rebuff, an act that occurs constantly in a tribe. It may be the highest and noblest act a wise man can perform. The very tale

of it, on the other hand, may be a matter for incredulous mirth, and the act itself impossible to conceive as a human possibility. Or it may be a crime punishable by law, or regarded as a sin against the gods.[3]

In *Patterns of Culture*, Benedict details the customs, values, and beliefs of three cultures. One of them is the culture of several groups of Indians of the Northwest Coast of America, mainly the Kwakiutl of Vancouver Island, whose traditional way of life survived until the end of the nineteenth century. Among those tribes it was an accepted practice to murder a man to acquire the rights to his name, his special dances, his personal crests, and his symbols. Similarly, when a loved one died, the mourners would search for someone of equal rank in a neighboring tribe, announce their intention of killing that person, and then proceed to do so. In this way, they vanquished fate and the pain of sorrow not by reacting passively, but by striking back.[4]

Another interesting culture described by Benedict is that of Dobu Island off the coast of New Guinea. At one time a cannibal culture, Dobu had "no chiefs . . . no political organization . . . no legality" when Benedict studied it. The Dobuan's entire life was spent in vicious competition. The rule of virtually every social enterprise was *cheat your neighbor*. The virtuous man, the respected man, was the one who had succeeded in injuring his rival in some way. Unlike the Northwest Coast Indian, the Dobuan who wished to rob or kill someone did not announce his plan but pretended affection and performed his treachery in secret or by surprise. The sorcery that the Dobuans practiced on one another was, in their view, made more potent by closeness to the victim.

So institutionalized had this practice become that the Dobu had a special term for it: *wabuwabu*, the achievement of "reap[ing] personal advantage in a situation in which others are victimized." Typical examples of *wabuwabu* were promising to trade the same valuable possession to several traders and breaking an engagement for marriage after obtaining the usual property settlement from the father of the betrothed. Given the unrelenting emphasis on the ill-treatment of others, it is not surprising that the Dobuans scorned laughter and "refrain[ed]" from pleasurable activities or expressions of happiness.[5]

During the mid-1960s, another anthropologist, Colin Turnbull, conducted an in-depth field study of an equally fascinating culture, that of the Ik tribe of Central Africa. The Ik acknowledge no moral or social obligation to anyone or anything. Their standard of value is the self; their rule of life, to do whatever they wish. At age 3, children are put out of their parents' huts and thereafter sleep in the open, rain or shine. To survive, they gather in bands and form not friendships but temporary alliances, which are betrayed whenever convenience dictates. Not surprisingly, children learn to cry tears of malice, anger, or hate, but never of sorrow. Because family life and community are foreign to their world, the Ik live out their lives without ever experiencing love, affection, or a sense of belonging, painfully aware that if illness or age weakens them, they will be left to die.

The Ik's sexual expression is typically adulterous and is driven less by passion than by the desire to profit at someone else's expense. A neighbor's suffering evokes not pity or kindness but malicious glee. On one occasion observed by Turnbull, when an emaciated little girl lay dying of hunger, her playmates put a bit of food in her hand and then, as she raised it to her mouth, beat her savagely. Similarly, mothers laugh when their infants fall and hurt themselves; if a leopard carries off a child, the parents' reaction is delight.

From the beginning of Turnbull's stay, he searched the tribe's daily behavior for some small evidence of love, some gesture of self-sacrifice for a loved one or a principle. He found none, although he did find "ample evidence" in their language and oral traditions that they had at one time known the meaning of values such as goodness and happiness. Turnbull concluded that the Ik had at some time abandoned their humanity for an existence of passionless mutual exploitation.[6]

□ INTERPRETING THE DIFFERENCES

What do anthropologists make of such differences between the traditional moral standards of our culture and the standards of the Kwakiutl, Dobuan, and Ik? What conclusions do anthropologists draw about the appropriateness of judging other cultures? The principle that has governed such matters is a complex and, in some ways, controversial principle known as *cultural relativity*. It derives from observation of cultural differences and two important realizations: (1) that a culture's values, rituals, and customs reflect its geography, history, and socioeconomic circumstances and (2) that hasty or facile comparison of other cultures with one's own culture tends to thwart scholarly analysis and produce shallow or erroneous conclusions.

In themselves these realizations are truisms; no reasonable person would deny that a people's experience influences its beliefs and behaviors or that careful, objective thinking is preferable to careless, biased thinking. Difficulty has arisen only because some anthropologists (and many other individuals) have leaped from these realizations to the conclusion that *whatever a culture considers morally acceptable is by that very fact morally acceptable.* Two facts about this conclusion are noteworthy. First, it is closely related to the majoritarian view discussed in Chapter 2 and has the same flaws. Also, this conclusion represents a crossing from one academic domain to another, from anthropology to ethics. Since academic boundaries are not well marked, such wandering is not uncommon. Unfortunately, it tends to compromise the quality of both scholarly and popular discussion. That is exactly what has happened in the case of cultural relativism.

Some anthropologists have challenged extreme interpretations of cultural relativity. Clyde Kluckhohn, for example, argues that "the principle of cultural relativity does not mean that because the members of some savage tribe are allowed to behave in a certain way that this fact gives intellectual warrant for such behavior in all groups. Cultural relativity means, on the contrary, that the appropriateness of any positive or negative custom must be evaluated with regard to how this habit fits with other group habits."[7] However, this argument merely adds a condition of consistency to the formula, saying, in effect, "whatever a group decides is moral will be moral *as long as it is consistent with other behaviors of the group.*" It leaves unanswered the very relevant question, "Is it possible for a custom or habit within a culture to be long-standing and completely consistent with other behaviors of the group *yet at the same time be immoral?*" Before addressing that question, let us balance our discussion of the differing values among cultures with consideration of similarities.

□ THE SIMILARITY OF VALUES

Modern anthropologists have found that it is all too easy to misinterpret the behaviors of people in other cultures. One way to misinterpret is to assume that something is not valued when *it is merely honored in a way we are not familiar with.* Clyde Kluckhohn cites an example from World War II. The behavior of some Japanese captives confounded American military men. On occasion, the same Japanese who had demonstrated fanatical allegiance to their emperor by risking their lives in suicide missions would, after being captured, write propaganda for the Americans, reveal information about Japanese bases, and even fly reconnaissance missions against their own people! To many American observers, those Japanese must have seemed to lack any sense of loyalty. Indeed, their behavior must have seemed cowardly and immoral. Yet to anthropologists familiar with the Japanese ethical system, Kluckhohn notes, the behavior was not mysterious at all. Their moral code required them to serve faithfully whatever authority under whose control they found themselves. When they were captured by the enemies of their country, they were obligated to transfer their allegiance from their emperor and military commanders to their captors. Although this was neither pleasant nor easy to do, their sense of honor required it.[8]

Another way to misinterpret other cultures is to assume a value is absent when, in fact, *it is merely subordinated to another, higher value.* To the casual observer, for example, the Hindus' refusal to use cattle to feed starving people shows a wanton disregard for human life. Yet the real explanation for the refusal is that their religion prevents them from butchering cattle for any purpose. A third way to misinterpret other cultures is to assume that a value is absent when *it is merely considered inapplicable to the situation in question.* Consider two cases mentioned earlier in the chapter: the man who helped his relative steal and the headhunters who replenished their supply of names. Although it certainly seemed that they were acting without a sense of justice or fairness, both were in fact acting on the idea that outsiders, people alien to their family or tribe, are "beyond the pale of moral consideration."[9] Justice and fairness are seen as inapplicable to them: They are not persons; hence, they have no rights. (If such reasoning seems bizarre, remember that many American slaveowners had similar attitudes toward their slaves, and that the domestic and foreign policies of "civilized" countries do not always, even to this day, coincide.)

The conclusion that even these brief examples suggest is that though behavior may vary greatly from culture to culture, the underlying values are, as a rule, remarkably similar. We find justice and courage, respect for one's relatives and tribal members, subordination of individual whim to custom or the judgments of tribal sages. If it is a mistake to deny the differences in human values, as manifested in the aberrant behaviors of the Ik and the Dobuans, then surely it is an even greater mistake to deny the similarities. Even the supposed gulf between Eastern and Western cultures is more apparent than real. In 1967 at the Aspen Institute of Humanistic Studies a famous Oriental scholar, Wing-sit Chan, and a famous Occidental scholar, Mortimer Adler, conducted a joint seminar. After reviewing the teachings of Confucius and Aristotle, and noting similarities and differences, seminar participants agreed that the main differences were style and method. Further, "it seemed equally clear to all present that the fundamental notions and insights were either the same or closely parallel."[10] Adler also rejects "the illusion that there is a Western mind and an Eastern mind, a European mind and an African mind, or a civilized mind and a primitive mind." In his view, "there is only a human mind and it is one and the same in all human beings."[11] In other words, all people have the same basic physiological, psychological, and intellectual equipment. They receive data from the same five senses; react with the same range of emotions; form attitudes, desires, dispositions, and intentions in the same ways; form ideas in the same manner; and even make the same kinds of mistakes—for example, overgeneralizing, oversimplifying, and jumping to conclusions.

□ IS JUDGMENT APPROPRIATE?

We have noted that people who accept an extreme interpretation of cultural relativism say that moral judgment of other cultures is never appropriate. We have also noted that multiculturalism extends that viewpoint to *subcultures*. In other words, multiculturalism clearly implies that within the larger American culture, Jews should not comment on the behavior of Protestants and neither of these groups should criticize the actions of Roman Catholics. Similarly, African Americans should remain silent about the behavior of Asian or European Americans, and vice versa. And Lithuanian Americans, Japanese Americans, and Peruvian Americans ought to remain mutually mute on moral issues outside their own ethnic groups. By this logic, your author, an Irish-Italian Caucasian American, has no business writing this book for a general audience. But then again, by the same logic, no one else has either!

This point of view may sound reasonable when presented in the abstract, but the moment we apply it to concrete cases, its shallowness becomes evident. What is wrong with African Americans denouncing white racism, Jews denouncing Nation of Islam leader Louis Farrakhan's anti-Semitic statements, Arabs and Christians denouncing the assassination of Israel's Prime Minister Rabin, and people all over the world denouncing apartheid in South Africa, Saddam Hussein's invasion of Kuwait, and the atrocities committed in Bosnia? The answer, most reasonable people would agree, is *nothing at all*. Such judgments are not only appropriate, but also morally responsible.

In some cases, we cannot avoid making moral judgments even if we try. In a 1973 decision (*Roe v. Wade*), the United States Supreme Court declared that the human fetus is not entitled to the protection of the law and abortion is therefore legal. Yet in 1975 the Constitutional Court of Germany reached the exact opposite legal opinion—that "the life of each individual human being is self-evidently a central value of the legal order . . . [and] the constitutional duty to protect this life also includes its preliminary stages before birth." The German high court reaffirmed this view in 1993, holding that the state has "a duty to place itself protectively before unborn human life, shielding this life from unlawful attacks" and calling for penal laws against anyone who would pressure pregnant women into having abortions.[12] *Holding either of these views necessarily entails rejecting the other.* We may, of course, try to reconcile the two views in the manner of cultural relativists or multiculturalists, but we will encounter mind-boggling difficulties. If a pregnant American woman visits Germany, for example, does her fetus magically gain moral and legal rights when the plane lands in Frankfurt? And what of the woman's German counterpart? Does her fetus leave Hamburg a person and arrive in New York a nonperson?

Earlier in this chapter we asked, but postponed answering, this question: "Is it possible for a custom or habit within a culture to be long-standing and completely consistent with other behaviors of the group *yet at the same time be immoral?*" History answers in the affirmative. Every age has moral issues that challenge all thinking, caring people, regardless of their race, creed, or ethnic heritage. During World War II, for example, the Nazis invaded their neighbors, hauled off many millions of people to concentration camps, performed hideous experiments without anesthetics, and performed mass executions. For the Allies to have ignored these heinous deeds on the grounds that whatever was approved in Nazi Germany was morally acceptable for Nazi Germany would have violated the memory of the Nazis' victims. When the war was finally won, the Allies, to their credit, held the famous Nuremberg trials, at which the responsible individuals were called to account for their "crimes against humanity." The United Nations based its well-known Declaration of Human Rights on essentially the same idea—that some actions deserve condemnation no matter where, when, or in what cultural circumstances they are performed and that no decent person or nation will shrink from condemning them.

The key to appreciating the appropriateness and, in some cases, the necessity of making moral judgments about other cultures and subcultures is to acknowledge three facts. The first is that cultures are dynamic rather than static (though the rate at which change occurs may vary greatly). Ancestral behaviors are not always mindlessly repeated but are often evaluated, embellished, refined, and/or reformed. Over time, the resulting changes can be significant. (Remember Colin Turnbull's observation that the Ik tribe at one time had a more civilized moral code but for some reason abandoned it.) Also, if a culture has contact with the outside world, some borrowing of ideas, beliefs, and values from other cultures is inevitable. Modern communications technology has provided unprecedented opportunities for intercultural borrowing. Communications satellites enable people in remote areas to receive television programs from any country. Personal computers, fax modems, and access to the Internet invite global exchange of ideas.

The second fact to be acknowledged is that the revolution in communications technology has profoundly altered the process by which cultural values are reaffirmed or modified and imparted to subsequent generations. Historically, those values were acquired in the home, the church, and the school, agencies that, though far from perfect, nevertheless took the welfare of children and society very seriously. In technologically advanced countries, the entertainment and communications media have become more influential than these agencies. American youngsters, for example, spend roughly twice as much time watching television as they do in the classroom and countless more hours listening to CDs and playing video games; they also see more than three-quarters of a million commercials and print advertisements by age 18. Moreover, the media are driven more by the desire for profit than by commitment to truth, dedication to moral excellence, or concern for the emotional and intellectual welfare of the public. Accordingly, as ratings competition has increased, the media have not hesitated to embrace sensationalism and glamorize ideas, attitudes, and values that directly oppose the teachings of home, church, and school. The mass culture (also known as popular culture) is being exported to virtually every corner of the world; and wherever it goes, it tends to undermine the traditional culture.

The third and most important fact, so obvious that theorists often overlook it, is that all of the people referred to in the previous two paragraphs are fallible creatures. This includes the ancestors who formulated cultural customs and moral codes; the progeny who preserved or changed those customs and codes; the parents, teachers, and clergy who perpetuate them; and the purveyors of mass culture who challenge them. At times these people will have made the effort to become well informed and will have raised important questions about issues, reasoned carefully and well, and produced genuine insights. Yet at other times their emotions, preconceptions, and assumptions will have biased their thinking and will have resulted in shallow or erroneous conclusions. The only way we have of determining which customs, codes, beliefs, values, and behaviors are wise and which are foolish is to examine them carefully and judge them honestly and fairly. The notion that other people's cultures (or our own culture) have in some mystical way escaped the effects of human fallibility does a disservice to the subject of ethics and to the men and women in every culture who have striven for moral excellence.

□ THREE IMPORTANT CAUTIONS

To say that moral judgment of other cultures is appropriate or necessary is not to say that it should be undertaken casually. To ensure that your judgments are fair and reasonable, keep these cautions in mind:

1. *Understanding is no substitute for moral judgment.* Since speaking from ignorance is irresponsible, we should refrain from judging any act until we understand the context in which it occurred. However, we should also avoid the mistake of ending our inquiry when we reach that understanding. An example will illustrate how this mistake occurs. Suppose we encounter a reference to the ancient Spartan practice of whipping young boys viciously. Resisting the temptation to judge without fuller understanding, we inquire further and learn that the whipping was part of a ritual marking the boy's initiation into manhood and that it symbolized the physical toughness required of a citizen in a warrior state. Our curiosity about context thus satisfied, we may have the vague feeling that we have settled the moral question *when all we have really done is sharpened its focus.* We now need to find out whether the ritual initiation of young boys into manhood by viciously whipping them was a moral practice.

    The details of what was done, the cultural situation in which it occurred, and the motivation of the person doing it are all very useful kinds of knowledge, but they are not the same as knowledge of the moral quality of the action itself. That kind of knowledge is the most important kind in ethics.

2. *The time and place of an act have no bearing on its moral quality.* Actions we would unhesitatingly denounce in our own time and place have a way of sounding morally acceptable for other times and places. If CNN reported that ritual human sacrifices had been performed last week in Kansas City to ensure a good harvest, we would be outraged and alarmed. But when we are told that many ancient cultures slaughtered people to ensure a good harvest, to dedicate a new temple, or to provide servants for a deceased monarch in the afterlife, our reaction may be "Oh, that's interesting." In such cases, we are tricked into attaching more significance to incidental details of time and place than to essential matters, as if the subtraction of a few centuries or even millennia, a geographical shift, and the adding of strange costumes and undecipherable incantations could transform an immoral act into a moral one (or vice versa). They cannot. The moral quality of an act remains the same whenever and wherever it occurs.

3. *Culpability for immoral acts may vary widely.* Culpability is moral responsibility or blame. Most people are familiar with the concept

as it applies in law. They know that taking another person's life warrants the death penalty or life imprisonment if the act was premeditated, a term of perhaps twenty years if it was committed in a moment of passion, and no punishment at all if it was done in self-defense. Although the act is identical in all three cases, the responsibility of the perpetrators varies according to the circumstances. The concept of culpability is equally important in ethics and will be discussed again in a later chapter. It is mentioned here only to show the importance of separating our judgment of any action from our determination of the culpability of the person who performs it. In some cases, the fairest judgment may be that the act is heinous but circumstances lessen the responsibility of the perpetrators. For example, we may denounce the cannibalism of a primitive tribe yet conclude that their contact with more civilized tribes was so limited and their moral lights were so dim that their culpability is significantly diminished. That would be a far more reasonable view than to confuse the act and the perpetrators and end up arguing that because they know no better their cannibalism is a moral practice.

▨ INQUIRIES *Do One of the following!*

1. In each of the following cases, the behavior illustrated seems to suggest that the people's values differ significantly from our own. Consider the possibility that, beneath appearances, the values are similar. Develop a plausible explanation for the difference in behavior.

a. In one culture, the elderly and those with severe handicaps are put to death. It would appear that this culture does not recognize human dignity as a value.

b. In another culture, this habit is observed: A person will ask a relative to do a task that requires days of labor and, when it is completed, never even thank the relative. On the other hand, if a stranger renders anyone the slightest service, the stranger is lavishly rewarded. It would appear that a sense of fairness is lacking in this culture.

c. Members of a tribe living in a remote jungle area commonly shun the sick. The moment members of the tribe become seriously ill, they cease to exist in the tribe's view. They must leave the village and care for themselves. If they recover, however, they are restored to tribal membership. Apparently, the tribe lacks compassion for the afflicted.

d.   A group of young boys are gathered together. Several men approach them, brandishing sticks and whips. They beat the boys viciously. The other male members of the tribe sit by and watch, laughing and obviously enjoying the event. It would seem that the men of this culture are sadistic, deriving pleasure from seeing others in pain.

e.   Whenever hunters in a certain culture are asked how their day's hunting went, they say "very well" and go on to declare that their relatives and friends and ancestors will be pleased with them. They say this whether they return heavily laden or empty-handed. It appears that truth-telling has no value in this culture.

f.   One woman finds another eating a piece of wild fruit. She calls to her neighbors and they stone the offender to death. Since the punishment does not fit the crime, it would appear that this culture lacks a sense of proportion and fails to recognize the value of human life.

g.   In an island culture, the men are seen returning from a fishing expedition. One man runs his canoe happily up on the beach. The villagers cheer him. Then a second canoe arrives. The second fisherman leaps out, runs to the first man, seizes his basket of fish, and throws it into the sea. He goes unpunished. The tribe seems to tolerate stealing.

h.   In some technologically advanced cultures, young people are "tracked" early in life to certain vocations and training programs. As adults, they have few career options and are expected to follow a path chosen for them. Apparently, the culture does not value self-determination and individual well-being.

  2.   When Hua, a Chinese woman, gave birth to a daughter rather than a son, her husband refused to look at the child. Later he punished his wife for the "offense" by withholding money and hitting her without provocation. When the child contracted pneumonia, he suggested she be left to die. Eventually, he divorced his wife—the decree cited his disapproval of having a girl baby and specified that the wife would keep the child and he would get their apartment. This story is not that uncommon in China, where masculinity is defined as producing a son to maintain the family line. This cultural value is so ancient and so strong that it is even reflected in the language— the character for the word *good* is a combination of the sign for "woman" and the sign for "son."[13] Evaluate this cultural value.

3. Earlier in this century Soviet dictator Joseph Stalin ordered the killing of 30 million peasants and filled the gulags (forced labor camps) with another 15 million, many of them guilty of nothing more than publicly disagreeing with his policies. Some people would say it is inappropriate for us to judge the morality of Stalin's actions because they took place in a different culture and at a different time. How would you answer them?

4. In some cultures mutilation is considered an appropriate punishment for certain crimes. For example, if a man is caught stealing, his hand is cut off. Since such a punishment is unheard of in our culture, we tend to consider it morally insupportable. Do you agree or disagree with this moral assessment?

5. At the beginning of the Persian Gulf crisis, Iraq's president, Saddam Hussein, held several thousand civilian hostages (he called them "guests") against their will and even moved them to military bases to deter attack by the United States and others. Hussein and many other Iraqis considered this action morally acceptable, whereas most Westerners considered it morally reprehensible. Is one view more justifiable than the other? Explain.

6. Imelda Marcos, wife of former Philippine dictator Ferdinand Marcos, reportedly spent millions on antiques in a single day. When her husband was deposed, her closet was found to contain 3,000 pairs of shoes and hundreds of priceless gowns. All this at a time when most of the people of that country lived in poverty. Since her culture is not our culture, is it proper for us to judge the morality of her actions? If so, what is your judgment? If not, why not?

7. The Eskimo husband's sense of hospitality requires him to offer his wife to an overnight guest. In our culture this is considered wrong. Is one view more justifiable than the other? Explain your reasoning carefully.

8. The case of the Japanese fliers detailed in this chapter reveals a different view of allegiance to authority than we are accustomed to. If American fliers were captured by the Japanese, we would have expected them to retain their loyalty to the United States rather than transfer it to their captors. Is one of these views more justifiable? Explain.

9. In some ancient cultures a young maiden was sacrificed each year to ensure a good harvest. In others, when the king died, many servants were killed and buried with him so that his needs in the afterlife could be suitably attended. Such practices are understandable, given the beliefs of the people. Are they morally right? Why or why not?

10. In ancient Rome, Sparta, and China, defective children and unwanted children were abandoned to die. Comment on the morality of this practice.

11. In some cultures a person who kills someone by accident must support the victim's family thereafter. In our culture we expect life insurance and social security to cover the family's needs. If the one responsible for the accident is found to be legally blameless, he or she is customarily considered morally blameless as well. Compare and evaluate these moral views.

12. Review the Dobuan moral code and underlying view of life presented in this chapter. To what extent is the code ethically justifiable?

13. When a Christian missionary is sent to preach the Gospel to members of a newly discovered tribe, she has the following experiences:

a. After arriving in their primitive jungle settlement and establishing a friendly relationship with them, she learns that they encourage extramarital promiscuity. She believes that this is morally wrong. She therefore explains to them that such promiscuity is immoral, an offense against God. Is the missionary's action ethical?

b. The same Christian missionary next learns that once each year, as an inducement to the god of the hunt to smile upon their efforts, members of the tribe cut off someone's right hand. (Whose right hand is determined quite democratically, by lottery.) The missionary is appalled by this custom and explains to the tribe that it is based on pure superstition. Is the missionary's action justifiable?

c. The missionary now makes an even more startling discovery. Since tribe members believe women are inferior to men and a tribe with a large number of women is an outrage to the god of good sense, they strictly control the female population. Whenever the number of girl babies exceeds the percentage approved by the wise men of the tribe, they permit no more girl babies born that year to live. More specifically, they take newborn babies out into the wilderness to die. The missionary tries to persuade them that such behavior is wrong. Is this action justifiable? Does your answer to this question agree with your answers to the first two questions? If not, explain why.

II

A STRATEGY

CHAPTER SIX

A FOUNDATION FOR JUDGMENT

If both individuals and cultures can be mistaken in their moral reasoning, we need a basis for evaluating their judgment. If the majority view, feelings, and conscience do not provide that basis, what does?

The first fact to note about our search for a surer foundation for moral judgment than the majority view, feelings, or conscience is that some philosophers say no such foundation exists! This skeptical assessment can be traced to the eighteenth-century English philosopher David Hume, who argued that there is no logical way to get from knowing what *is* (factual knowledge) to knowing what *ought to be* (objective moral standards). In other words, Hume held that no amount of observation of the way people actually behave can ever lead to a conclusion about the way they should behave. Hume's view of this issue profoundly influenced English and American thought and continues to challenge contemporary philosophers.

We will begin by asking some probing questions about Hume's conclusion. If you feel somewhat uncomfortable about questioning the ideas advanced by scholars of Hume's rank, be assured that such apprehension is natural enough and, to some extent, healthy. Respect for revered thinkers is a desirable quality. *But respect for people does not demand endorsement of their ideas; it only requires acknowledgment of their integrity.* The best tribute we can pay to the great thinkers of the past is to examine their ideas with the same passion for truth and rigorous analysis they displayed.

□ SOME HISTORICAL EXAMPLES

Our first query concerns whether the sages of ancient and modern societies have avoided moral prescriptions in the manner of Hume. In the vast majority of cases (very possibly, *all* of them), the answer is no. Virtually every society, ancient and modern, has formulated moral prescriptions—oughts—for the guidance of its members. Here are but a few examples. (In the last three instances, the *ought* is not stated directly but is clearly implied.)

> Slander not. (Babylonian)
>
> One should never strike a woman; not even with a flower. (Hindu)
>
> He who is asked for alms should always give. (Hindu)
>
> Never do to others what you would not like them to do to you. (Chinese)
>
> The Master said, Respect the young. (Chinese)
>
> Love thy wife studiously. Gladden her heart all thy life long. (Ancient Egyptian)
>
> Be blameless to thy kindred. Take no vengeance even though they do thee wrong. (Old Norse)
>
> Choose loss rather than shameful gains. (Greek)
>
> Death is to be chosen before slavery and base deeds. (Roman)
>
> Nature and Reason command that nothing uncomely . . . [and] nothing lascivious be done or thought. (Roman)
>
> Let him not desire to die, let him not desire to live, let him wait for his time . . . let him patiently bear hard words, entirely abstaining from bodily pleasures. (Ancient Indian)
>
> I sought no trickery, nor swore false oaths. (Anglo-Saxon)
>
> In the Dalebura tribe a woman, a cripple from birth, was carried about by the tribespeople in turn until her death at the age of sixty-six. . . . They never desert the sick. (Australian Aborigines)
>
> You will see them take care of . . . widows, orphans, and old men, never reproaching them. (Native American)[1]

□ THE FOUNDING FATHERS' MORAL JUDGMENT

Our next question is whether the Founding Fathers of the United States accepted Hume's view and avoided making moral judgments. In this case, too, the answer is that they did not. The Declaration of Independence begins with the moral judgments that "all Men are created equal, that they are endowed by their Creator with certain unalienable Rights, that among these are Life, Liberty, and the Pursuit of Happiness"; further, it states that the people empower the government to "secure these Rights" and when the government fails to do so, the people have not only a right but also a duty to overthrow it. The Declaration proceeds to present a lengthy list of "Injuries and Usurpations"—that is, moral offenses—allegedly committed by King George against the colonists. The United States Constitution was created out of that same moral frame of reference. The Bill of Rights, in fact, is properly viewed as a safeguard that the moral obligations affirmed in the Declaration of Independence would not be violated. Its preamble makes clear that the amendments were proposed "in order to prevent mis-construction or abuse of its [that is, the Constitution's] powers. . . ."

□ ETHICAL CODES IN ORGANIZATIONS

Our third question is whether corporations and communities of scholars, following Hume's reasoning, refrain from establishing moral norms to govern their internal and external relationships. Here, too, the answer is that they do not. Virtually every sizeable corporation has a carefully framed code of ethics. The same is true of virtually every professional organization, including the American Academy of Forensic Sciences, the American Institute of Chemists, the American Pharmaceutical Society, the American Psychological Association, the American Society of Zoologists, and the American Medical Association. (A notable exception is the American Philosophical Association, which has no published code of ethics. This situation is ironic since ethics has historically been a subdiscipline of philosophy.)

The American Sociological Association's Code of Ethics, to cite a typical example, sets guidelines for the practice of sociology, for the review process in publishing, and for teaching and supervision. The preamble affirms that the activities of the discipline are "social processes involving ethical considerations and behavior at every stage" and encourages sociologists to "educate themselves and their colleagues to behave ethically."[2] The Code is filled with *should*s and *must*s and *obligation*s—the language of *ought*. For example, it proclaims that sociologists

"should strive to maintain objectivity"
"have the obligation to disseminate their research findings"
"should not misuse their positions"

"must acknowledge all persons who contribute to their research"

"must refrain from exploiting students"

"should [never] discriminate in hiring, firing, promotions"

□ MORAL JUDGMENT IN EVERYDAY LIFE

So far we have noted that most (and conceivably, all) societies both before and since Hume's time have not hesitated to formulate general moral standards, that moral judgments are woven into the fabric of the U.S. Declaration of Independence and the Constitution, and that virtually every business and professional organization has a specific moral code that is considered binding on its members. Our final question concerns whether the average person accepts Hume's dictum and refrains from judging the ethical issues he or she personally encounters in everyday life or finds in the news of the day. The answer here is consistent with our answers in the other cases: No.

A single case will serve to illustrate how easily and naturally moral judgment occurs. Millions of people around the world followed the story of Susan Smith, the South Carolina woman who rolled her car into a lake with her two young children strapped inside and then concocted a story about a kidnapping, complete with pleas for their safe return, encouragements to the children to be brave, and public prayers. The overwhelming reaction to her confession of guilt was moral outrage. International analysis of the case produced millions of words of commentary, but to this writer's knowledge not a single writer or speaker acknowledged any difficulty deciding the moral quality of Susan Smith's action. Tens of millions of people from Spain to Sri Lanka, Helsinki to Hoboken, held the same unshakable conviction—that if Susan Smith no longer loved her children she should have surrendered custody to her husband or given the children up for adoption instead of murdering them.

The facts we have considered represent valuable circumstantial evidence against Hume's view that is logically impossible to get from *is* to *ought*. They make clear that if Hume was right then most people, most organizations, most societies throughout history have been wrong. We are justified in thinking this highly unlikely, yet we cannot say that it is *impossible*. Individuals are no less fallible in large groups than alone, and under certain circumstances illogical thinking can be contagious. Therefore, it would be a mistake to believe that our facts have disproved Hume's view; they have only raised doubts about it. In order to make the case that

Hume is wrong and moral prescriptions can be legitimately made, we will have to demonstrate that there is a way to get from *is* to *ought*.

□ THE PRINCIPLE OF RIGHT DESIRE

Like it or not, each of us must make dozens of moral choices daily. Will we go to work or call in sick? Follow the research protocol or violate it? Put quotes around borrowed phrasing or pretend the words are our own? Answer a colleague's question truthfully or lie? Stop for the red light or go through it? Pay the bills or spend the money on entertainment instead? Respond to our spouse's need for appreciation and affection or ignore it? Pet the cat or kick it? Find time to communicate with our children or rebuff them? In such cases, we are free to respond as we choose, but we are not free to avoid responding. And however wisely or foolishly we choose, each response will say more than "This is what I am doing because this is what I am doing"—it will say "I consider this choice preferable to all other possibilities" or "I know this is not preferable but I'm going to do it anyway," which also acknowledges that one way is preferable. Regardless of how we define "preferable" in any particular case—less troublesome, more enjoyable, in our interest, or some other way—the underlying assumption will always be the same: that we *ought* to do what is preferable.

The critical question is, Is this assumption logically justifiable? One of the foremost interpreters of the Western intellectual tradition, Mortimer Adler, maintains that it is. The kind of truth applicable to moral questions, Adler maintains, is not "correspondence with the way things really are" but "conformity with right desire"; further, there are two types of desire, acquired and natural—the former represented by the *wants* that differ from individual to individual, and the latter by the *needs* that all human beings have in common. The process of reaching conclusions about good and evil and right behavior, in Adler's view, produces "a body of respectable knowledge."[3] What can we say with confidence that we ought to desire and pursue? In *philosophical* terms, Adler responds that we should desire what is *really* good for us (as opposed to what is only apparently good for us or what we merely desire). Adler has concluded that "the only self-evident principle in the sphere of desire, the only truly categorical imperative," is that *"We ought to desire everything really good for us and nothing else."*[4]

Saying the principle of desire is self-evident means that its opposite—
that we should want what is bad for us or not want what is good for us—
is inconceivable. In other words, it means that the principle is beyond
question, indisputable, precisely the qualities necessary to solve the
is/ought problem. Failure to recognize that moral truth consists of conformity to right desire prevented Hume and his followers from acknowledging the principle and thus solving the problem. (Incidentally, Aristotle
expressed this insight two thousand years earlier but in Hume's time,
Aristotle's writings were no longer in fashion.) With this principle as our
major premise, Alder explains, we can establish moral prescriptions or
norms, in this manner:[5]

> We ought to desire what is really good for us.
> Knowledge is really good for us.
> We ought to desire knowledge.

The premise "knowledge is really good for us," of course, like any
other premise inserted in that position, cannot be assumed to be true; its
truth must be demonstrated. But if this can be accomplished, the conclusion is inescapable. Skeptics may object that the kind of demonstration that
can be made for statements of what is good for us does not provide
absolute, scientific certainty and is therefore unacceptable. But this argument requires ethics to meet a more stringent standard than other disciplines. Every day in virtually every academic field, including the sciences,
a lesser standard than certainty is accepted. For example, Darwin's theory
of evolution is taught as fact despite science's failure to find the "missing
link," and the scientific community endorses the idea that cigarette smoking can cause lung cancer without absolutely conclusive evidence.
Similarly, assertions are made about the origin of the universe despite the
fact that the reality in question has never been, and indeed may never be,
known with certainty. Whenever certainty is unachievable in these and
other academic fields, the less demanding standard of *probability* is considered adequate. Fairness demands that the subject of ethics should be
treated no differently.

☐ THE PRINCIPLE OF CONTRADICTION

One of the most dramatic ethical issues of the millennium has exploded
during the final decade of the twentieth century. That issue is the creation

of human embryos for research. Advances in medical technology have made possible *in vitro* fertilization, which unites sperm and egg outside the female body in a test tube. The initial intention of this technology was to accomplish pregnancy for couples who, for medical reasons, could not conceive a child in the natural way. The fertilized egg would be implanted in the woman's uterus and the pregnancy would proceed. In a proposed controversial use, an egg would be fertilized in a test tube, allowed to develop into an embryo, used for scientific experimentation, *and then discarded after fourteen days,* the point at which the embryo's nervous system begins to function. The procedure was unanimously recommended by a National Institutes of Health advisory committee, the Human Embryo Research Panel. The committee stated that such research would improve infertility treatment, provide new methods for birth control, new cancer therapies, and increased understanding of birth defects. (Aware of the controversial nature of the proposal, President Bill Clinton imposed a ban on federal funding of the research.)[6]

A *Washington Post* editorial denounced the panel's recommendation, commenting that "The creation of human embryos specifically for research that will destroy them is unconscionable." And the Ramsey Colloquium, a group of Jewish and Christian theologians, philosophers, and scholars that meets periodically to consider questions of ethics, religion, and public life, issued a formal statement of opposition. The Ramsey statement concluded that the panel's recommendation "is morally repugnant, entails grave injustice to innocent human beings, and constitutes an assault upon the foundational ideals of human dignity and rights essential to a free and decent society." It also expressed concern that panel members are themselves engaged in the very research for which they are recommending funding, a situation that raises questions of conflict of interest.[7]

Controversial issues like this one often generate considerable intellectual tension. People form strong convictions on one side of the issue or the other and attempt to persuade others of the rightness of their viewpoint. Even relativists can be found arguing passionately for one side of an issue despite their professed belief that all views are equal. Underlying all such debates is a principle that both sides acknowledge, either consciously or unconsciously. In other words, whether or not they give verbal affirmation of the principle, whether or not they have conceptualized it, they attest to it by the very act of debating. This principle is known as the principle of contradiction and is expressed as follows: *An idea cannot be both true and false at the same time in the same way.*

The qualifying terms "at the same time" and "in the same way" are significant. If George died this morning, the sentence "George is alive" was true yesterday and is false today, yet it was *not true and false at the same time.* If one of your professors presents intellectually challenging ideas in a dull monotone, the sentence "That course is stimulating" is both true and false at the same time, yet *not in the same way.* Where we are dealing with a genuine contradiction, on the other hand, we can no more imagine both sides being true than we can imagine a stick with one end or a square circle.

Contradiction is not always blatant; sometimes it is subtle and thus may escape detection for years. For example, in the very same book in which he denounced the use of *never, always,* and similar terms denoting absolutes, Joseph Fletcher, the founder of "situation ethics" wrote "love is the only norm," and "no unwanted babies should ever be born."[8] Those are absolute statements. As one critic of situation ethics has pointed out, "Fletcher's claim that all is relative . . . is self-destructive. It says in effect, "we should never use the word never. Never! Or, we should always avoid using the word always. Always!" (Fletcher could have avoided this embarrassing problem by moderating his assertion, saying "Be careful in using words like *always* and *never.* Often they overstate the case.") This critic goes on to argue that the relativists' quandary is that they must either be absolutely sure that there are no absolutes, in which case they have contradicted themselves; or they are not absolutely sure, in which case they admit there may be absolutes.[9]

□ CHALLENGES TO JUDGMENT

The principle of right desire, in bridging the gap between *is* and *ought,* provides a foundation for judgment. The principle of contradiction gives assurance that critical thinking is relevant to ethical controversies, that when two ethical judgments are diametrically opposed, one must be mistaken. Thus, these two principles offer us confidence and encouragement in ethical analysis and judgment, no small contributions. They do not, however, answer the questions, What is really good for us? What criteria and approaches are most effective in examining moral issues? What pitfalls should we be aware of and strive to avoid? All these challenges will be the focus of subsequent chapters, but the third deserves preliminary consideration here.

In Greek legend sailors had to negotiate their ships between twin perils: Scylla, a female sea monster, and Charybdis, a deadly whirlpool. If they drifted too far to either the right or the left, they were doomed. Anyone who undertakes ethical analysis and judgment is similarly challenged to steer a course between the "monsters" of relativism and absolutism. Relativism, as we noted in Chapter 5, is the view that no objective moral standard is possible; hence, issues of right and wrong are personal and subjective and may be decided by each person for himself or herself without danger of being wrong. As the dominant moral perspective of our age, it claims more victims than its evil twin, but absolutism is no less dangerous for that fact.

Absolutism is the view that the circumstances of a case make no difference, that moral judgment consists solely in applying rigid, inflexible rules to cases. "Right is right, wrong is wrong, and qualifications of cases destroy morality" is the byword of the absolutist. An important distinction must be made between absolutism and the belief in moral absolutes, the view that some actions are always, or almost always, wrong. Many people tend to confuse the two and as a result feel that belief in moral absolutes automatically makes one narrow-minded and fanatical. That notion is mistaken. After the Nazi trials for crimes committed against humanity during World War II, the international community created the Nuremberg Code, which forbade experiments on human beings without their explicit consent; it also forbade experiments that exposed patients to unnecessary suffering, disabling injury, or risk of death even *with* their consent. The 1975 Helsinki Declaration of the World Medical Association stated: "Concern for the interests of the subject [used in research] must always prevail over the interest of science and society." Both the Nuremberg prohibition and the Helsinki Declaration's principle are moral absolutes, and both are almost universally accepted.

Clearly, *the acceptance of moral absolutes does not constitute absolutism.* In other words, one can believe in moral absolutes and still remain willing to consider new evidence and examine related cases fair-mindedly. Moreover, the quest for moral absolutes, norms that have broad and even universal application, is eminently reasonable. G. K. Chesterton lamented that progress ought to mean changing things around us to conform to our vision of what they ought to be, but in modern times it has come to mean continually changing our vision. "We are not altering the world to suit the ideal," he wrote. "We are [instead] altering the ideal: it is easier."[10] This tendency Chesterton regarded as a profound error; he reasoned that progress is possible only if the ideal is constant and unchanged: "Whistler used to make many rapid studies of a sitter; it did not matter if he tore up twenty portraits. But it would matter if he looked up twenty times, and each time saw a new person sitting placidly for his portrait."[11] In order to conduct moral discourse, we need some standard. The quest for moral absolutes, carefully conducted, is the obvious way to find such a standard.

In closing, let us return to the extreme perspectives of absolut*ism* and relativ*ism*. The problem with both these extremes is that they trivialize the subject of ethics. If, as the relativist believes, no objective moral standard is possible and everything is a matter of personal preference, then the terms *right* and *wrong* have little practical application and ethics is without real value. On the other hand, if as the absolutist believes, circumstances make no difference, then there is little point in studying the details of cases and making comparative studies of similar cases. Your challenge is to steer a course between relativism and absolutism. You are not likely to have a problem with both extremes; instead, you will undoubtedly be inclined toward one or the other. Determine now which one that is and try to assess its influence on your judgment. Whenever you are analyzing a moral issue, be alert to that influence and take whatever measures are necessary to overcome it.

⌘ INQUIRIES

1. Extend the list of historical examples of *oughts* by adding others that you learned at home, in school, or in church.

2. Consult the ethics code of an organization you belong to and are familiar with. If you don't belong to any organizations, visit the library and consult the code of a professional organization. List the main moral prescriptions included in that code. (*Note:* save your response to this inquiry; you will be asked to refer to it in a later chapter.)

3. Consult print and broadcast sources for one or more current news stories that, like the Susan Smith story, have evoked moral judgment from the general public. Summarize each story, describe the dominant public view of the moral issue involved, and then decide whether you agree with that view.

4. Examine each of the following ethical questions in light of what you have learned in this chapter and previous chapters. In each instance, answer the question and state the reasoning that led to that answer. (*Note:* save your response to this inquiry; you will be asked to refer to it in a later chapter.)

a. Copyright law makes it illegal to copy computer software programs. Yet sometimes students want or need a program that is too expensive for them to buy. In such cases, is it morally acceptable for students to copy a friend's software?

b. Often a person will work for someone, learn all the procedures, formulas, and strategies of the business, and then quit and take a job with a competitor or start a new, competing business. Is it morally acceptable for her to use what she learned on the previous job? To approach her previous employer's customers and try to persuade them to do business with her? To use her previous employer's "secrets" (recipes in the food industry, for example, or formulas in the cosmetic industry)?

c. Is it morally acceptable for store owners to include such subliminal messages as "Don't steal" in the music piped into the store? What about subliminal appeals ("Buy now") to spend money in the store?

d. Is drag racing on the highway ethical?

e. Is it morally right for old people to be put in institutions when their children have room for them in their homes?

f. Is it permissible to kill animals of an endangered species?

g. Is it ethical for the United States to train the police and military forces of dictatorships that use those forces to suppress their citizens?

h. Is it ethical for the United States to continue diplomatic relations with countries that deny women the basic rights of citizenship?

i. Is it morally acceptable for children to be used in pornographic films? Does it make a difference if their parents approve?

j. There are more than four hundred pet cemeteries in the United States. People often spend hundreds of dollars to bury their dogs, cats, birds, goldfish, and hamsters. Is this practice morally acceptable?

k.   Many countries employ secret agents, spies whose duty is to learn the military or diplomatic secrets of other countries. Is it morally permissible to be a secret agent? Is it morally permissible to be a double agent (one who works for both sides while pretending to work exclusively for each)?

CHAPTER SEVEN

THE BASIC CRITERIA

What is really good for us? What criteria and approaches are most effective in examining moral issues? What pitfalls other than relativism and absolutism should we be aware of and strive to avoid?

In previous chapters we noted that religion and law cannot substitute for ethics, although they are related to and compatible with ethics; that the majority view is as apt to be mistaken as correct; that feelings are often capricious and therefore unreliable; and that conscience, though in some cases trustworthy, is susceptible to negative influences and error. We also found that, contrary to popular opinion, moral judgments of other cultures are appropriate when they are based on understanding and thoughtful analysis. Finally, we observed that despite skepticism's claim that moral prescriptions ("ought" statements) are illogical, such prescriptions have been made throughout history and are still made by prestigious organizations; and even more important, we observed that the principle of right desire provides the necessary foundation in logic and, together with the principle of contradiction, enables us to approach ethical analysis with confidence. In this chapter we will build upon that foundation.

The standard we will need for judging the morality of actions is one that is acceptable to men and women of various moral perspectives and reflects the principles that most ethical systems have in common. Such a standard will help us to set aside defensiveness, free ourselves from the entanglements of prefabricated interpretations, and elevate our dialogue to a more analytic and objective level.

□ A FUNDAMENTAL GOOD: RESPECT FOR PERSONS

One example of something that is "really good for us," as we noted in the previous chapter, is knowledge. Another significant "good" is *respect for persons*, which, as Errol E. Harris explains, includes the following three requirements:

> First, that each and every person should be regarded as worthy of sympathetic consideration, and should be so treated; secondly, that no person should be regarded by another as a mere possession, or used as a mere instrument, or treated as a mere obstacle, to another's satisfaction; and thirdly, that persons are not and ought never to be treated in any undertaking as mere expendables.[1]

Respect for persons is an important value in most ethical systems. (The Dobuans and the Ik are noteworthy exceptions.) This is not to say that respect for persons is always interpreted in the same way or that it is always given precedence over other values. In some cultures "person" is defined not broadly, as "all members of the species *Homo sapiens*," but narrowly, as "a member of our tribe" or "one who enjoys the rights of citizenship." In the tribal languages of some headhunters and cannibals, the word used to denote a "person" is the tribal name; to be outside the tribe is thus, by definition, to be a nonperson. In the Roman Empire many of the freedoms now associated with personhood were denied to noncitizens, notably slaves. (Roman citizenship could, however, be bestowed on anyone, even a slave.) Yet even in such cultures, where personhood is more narrowly conceived, respect for persons is nevertheless honored.

One reason respect for persons has historically been, and continues to be, universally accepted is that it can be affirmed theologically as well as philosophically and is thus acceptable to believers and nonbelievers alike. In the philosophical sense, respect for persons may be considered an extension of the principle of right desire. Just as we should desire only what is really good for us, so too we should desire the same thing for other people because they are essentially no different from us. In the theological sense, respect for persons reinforces the idea that human beings are created in the image and likeness of God and are therefore, their many differences notwithstanding, children of God.

□ THREE BASIC CRITERIA

As the requirements stated by Errol Harris suggest, respect for persons is not merely a theoretical construct but a practical standard for the treatment of others in everday situations. Over the centuries three basic criteria have been associated with that standard and have informed ethical discourse. These criteria—*obligations, ideals,* and *consequences*—will be our principal concern in this chapter and subsequent chapters.

OBLIGATIONS

Every significant human action occurs, directly or indirectly, in a context of relationships with others. And relationships usually imply *obligations;* that is, restrictions on our behavior, demands to do something or to avoid doing it. The most obvious kind of obligation is a formal agreement. Whenever a person enters into a contract with someone—for example, to sell something or to perform a service—we consider that person ethically (as well as legally) bound to live up to his or her agreement.

There are other kinds of obligations, too. Obligations of friendship, for example, demand the keeping of confidences. Obligations of citizenship in a democracy demand concern for the conduct of government and responsible participation in the electoral process. There are business obligations. The employer or supervisor, for example, is morally bound to use fair hiring practices, judge workers impartially, and pay them a reasonable wage that is consistent with the demands of their position and the quality of their work. The employee, in turn, is morally bound to do a job as efficiently and competently as he or she is able to. Both have moral obligations to their customers.

In addition, there are professional obligations. Lawyers are obligated to protect the interests of their clients, doctors to promote or restore the health of their patients, teachers to advance the knowledge and wisdom of their students, elected officials to serve the interests of their constituents.

When we say obligations bind morally, we mean they exist to be honored. To honor them is right; to dishonor them is wrong. The fact that what is considered an obligation may be found to be illegitimate does not refute this idea. An illegitimate obligation is a contradiction in terms: If it is illegitimate, then it is not an obligation. Even if the action we are required or forbidden to perform is morally insignificant, the obligation has moral force. Thus, if Edna promises not to go to the carnival without notifying Carl in advance, to break the promise without a compelling reason is to do wrong. Surely there is nothing wrong in going to the carnival or in not calling Carl beforehand. It is the *promise* that binds Edna.

IDEALS

In the general sense *ideals* are notions of excellence, goals that bring greater harmony in one's self and between self and others. In ethics, ideals are also specific concepts that assist us in achieving respect for persons in our moral judgments. Some common ideals that figure prominently in ethical reasoning are fairness, tolerance, compassion, loyalty, forgiveness, amity, and peace.

Different cultures interpret the same ideal differently, of course. As we have seen, the way a culture interprets its ideals and relates one to another will affect its judgment of particular actions. The Eskimo accepts the ideal of respect for the aged, but some of the Eskimo's ways of honoring it—for instance, walling them up in an igloo to die when they are too old to contribute to the community and are a drain on its resources—are very different from ours. Furthermore, the same ideal of justice that we honor may impel someone in another culture to do something we would never think of doing: for instance, to cut out the tongue of one who has uttered a taboo word. These variations in the ways of viewing and pursuing ideals surely pose exquisite dilemmas for those engaged in cross-cultural studies and those whose occupations involve them directly with other cultures (diplomats, for example, and medical and religious missionaries). They present less difficulty for us in the examination of our own culture.

CONSEQUENCES

Consequences are the beneficial or harmful effects that result from an action and affect the people involved, including, of course, the person performing the action. Some consequences are physical; others are emotional. Some occur immediately; others occur only with the passing of time. Some are intended by the person performing the act; others are unintended. Finally, some consequences may be obvious, and others may be very subtle and hidden by appearances. The ethicist is concerned with all significant consequences of actions occurring in a moral context. Because consequences can be complex and difficult to pinpoint, ethical analysis very often requires not merely an examination of indisputable facts, but also speculation about possibilities and probabilities.

Generally speaking, then, a moral action is one that demonstrates respect for persons by honoring the relevant obligations and ideals and by producing favorable consequences.

□ ANALYZING ETHICAL ISSUES

As your analyses of the inquiries in previous chapters have undoubtedly revealed, the job of examining issues and making judgments can be a difficult one, even when the cases are relatively simple. The fact that you now have a set of criteria to use can be of considerable help to you if you apply the criteria thoughtfully and systematically. The following approach will help you accomplish this:

STEP 1: STUDY THE DETAILS OF THE CASE

Study the details of the case carefully. Look closely at any circumstances that set it apart from otherwise similar cases. Keep in mind that "circumstances alter cases." Suppose, for example, that a computer operator used her employer's computer for her own personal project. Is such an action morally acceptable? It is impossible to give a meaningful answer without knowing more of the details of the case. You must identify the important questions that a meaningful answer would depend upon. *Did she use the computer on her own time or on company time? Was she expressly forbidden to use it? Was her personal project in any way competitive with or harmful to her employer's business?* These are the key questions.

If, as often happens, you have insufficient details about a case to answer one or more of your important questions, speculate about *possible* answers. For example, if the issue were the firing of a teacher because of his homosexuality and you didn't know the specific cause of his being fired, you would consider the possibilities that (a) he was propagandizing for homosexuality in his class, (b) he was enticing his own students, and (c) he was merely living with another homosexual. For the first two causes the firing may be morally defensible, but for the third it would undoubtedly be indefensible.

STEP 2: IDENTIFY THE RELEVANT CRITERIA

Identify specific criteria that are relevant to the case. In other words, ask these questions: Are there any *obligations*? What *ideals* are involved? What are the *consequences* of the case? Whom will they affect? In what way? After identifying the criteria, decide where the emphasis should lie. Sometimes the issue will be mainly a matter of obligation; at other times an ideal will be most important; at still other times the consequences will be most important. Not infrequently, the force of all three will be very nearly equal.

STEP 3: DETERMINE POSSIBLE COURSES OF ACTION

Determine all possible choices of action that are (or, in the case of a past action, were) available. This consideration can have a significant bearing on the judgment of an action. Occasionally an action that would normally be considered immoral will be justifiable because no reasonable alternative course of action is available. For example, although the deliberate killing of an individual is wrong, a police officer is justified in shooting a berserk man who has taken a woman hostage and suddenly begins choking and stabbing her. More commonly, one or more alternative choices will be open to a person. By determining what they are, you increase your chances of making a reasonable moral judgment.

STEP 4: DECIDE WHICH ACTION IS MOST ETHICAL

In light of your findings in steps one through three, decide which action is most ethical.

This four-step approach will help you cut through the confusion that surrounds many complex moral issues, overcome indecision, and reach a judgment, and it will also help you express that judgment to others. Let's look at two cases and see how the approach works in practice.

☐ THE CASE OF AGATHA'S RELATIONSHIP

Agatha, a married woman with three children, is in the habit of seeing her unmarried minister alone rather often. Since the relationship began several years ago with a mutual interest in intellectual and social issues, it has grown and expanded. Agatha's daily visits to the minister's home and his frequent visits to hers, sometimes when her husband is at home, but often when he is not, have become the subject of community gossip and are threatening both their reputations. There has been no overt sexual dimension to the relationship; it has remained platonic. Lately, however, Agatha has begun to have sexual thoughts about the minister. Is it morally wrong for her to continue the relationship?

ANALYSIS 1: THE DETAILS OF THE CASE

You would note the details given and identify the following important questions, which are not answered in the statement of the case:

How old are the children?

How solid and mutually nourishing was Agatha's relationship with her husband before she began her relationship with the minister?

If there have been problems in her relationship with her husband, have they discussed them? Have they made any progress in solving them?

Has Agatha discussed with the minister the direction in which their relationship seems to be heading? If so, what was his reaction?

What other possibilities does Agatha have for social life and intellectual fulfillment?

ANALYSIS 2: RELEVANT CRITERIA

You would identify the obligations, ideals, and consequences involved in the case. There are several *obligations*. Agatha has an obligation to herself to exercise her intellect and realize her potential. As a wife she has an obligation to her husband (as he does to her) to build and nurture a mutually satisfying physical and emotional relationship. As a mother she has an obligation to provide a home and atmosphere conducive to her children's physical, emotional, moral, and intellectual development. The minister, too, has at least one relevant obligation—to serve his congregation's religious and spiritual needs.

At least two *ideals* are involved: marital fidelity and honesty with self and friends. (We might also note the traditional but now sometimes questioned ideal of the minister as a model of scandal-free behavior.) Marital fidelity has, of course, more dimensions than the sexual: A spouse can be faithful in body but not in mind, in attitude, in heart. The ideal of honesty with self demands that Agatha not deceive herself about the probable direction of her relationship with the minister.

What about the *consequences* of continuing the relationship? It is unlikely that Agatha's marriage will be strengthened by continuing it. In fact, the reverse is a distinct possibility. Her sexual thoughts could easily lead to sexual involvement, which would break her bond of faith with her husband and threaten her marriage. At the very least it would undoubtedly create (or increase) tension in her relationship with him. Even if that tension were never directly expressed and Agatha and her husband worked hard to be loving parents, the fact that the tension existed would affect the children indirectly.

Neither is the effect of the relationship on the minister's vocation likely to be beneficial. It could destroy his effectiveness as a minister and jeopardize his position, particularly if he belongs to a conservative religious denomination.

ANALYSIS 3: POSSIBLE COURSES OF ACTION

You would consider the possible actions open to Agatha and decide that she does not have to allow events to control her. She has several alternatives. She could end the platonic relationship with the minister, explaining to him that she is doing so to save her marriage. Or she could see him less frequently and never alone or in his or her home. (This would be more effective if it were combined with an attempt to renew her relationship with her husband and find other social and intellectual outlets.) On the other hand, she could obtain a legal separation from her husband.

ANALYSIS 4: THE MOST ETHICAL ACTION

In light of your analysis you would probably conclude that the three criteria—obligations, ideals, and consequences—are of nearly equal force and all of them suggest that it is wrong for Agatha to continue the relationship with the minister, at least in its present form, and that despite the satisfaction she and the minister get from it and despite the fact that it is not tainted with sexual infidelity, it does cause harm and will very likely cause additional harm in the future. Concerning which course of action is the most supportable on ethical grounds, you would probably reason as follows:

If Agatha's relationship with her husband was reasonably healthy before she met the minister, she should end the relationship with the minister or at least severely curtail it. If her relationship with her husband had already deteriorated and is beyond rebuilding, then she should consider leaving him. The age of her children should be a factor in the decision of whether to leave her husband. If she does leave, the possible effects of the scandal on the minister should influence her decision of whether to continue her relationship with him after leaving.

□ THE CASE OF HORACE'S HOUSE

Mr. Barker is returning to a town he once lived in and a position he once held. He and his wife visit several real estate brokers there in hopes of finding a house. One broker mentions that Horace's house will soon be for sale. "Oh," Barker says, "I know Horace; is he leaving the area?" The broker explains that he is not, but is moving to a larger house she showed him because his family has outgrown their present home. As they are driving to inspect Horace's property, Barker casually asks the broker which house Horace is buying. The broker tells him. She innocently adds that he is paying $78,000 for it.

After leaving the broker, Barker goes directly to the owner of the house Horace is planning to buy, inspects it, is impressed with what he sees, and says to the owner, "Look, I know Horace has offered you $78,000. I'll pay $79,000, and what's more, you won't have to pay any broker's commission." The owner agrees and Barker buys the house. Was Barker's behavior unethical?

ANALYSIS 1: THE DETAILS OF THE CASE

After a close reading of this case, you would probably decide that, unlike the case of Agatha's relationship, the statement of this case leaves no significant questions unanswered.

ANALYSIS 2: RELEVANT CRITERIA

Whether Barker violated a *legal* obligation between the broker and the owner of the house is a question that does not concern us here. But did he violate a *moral obligation*? Clearly, the broker did not give him the information so that he could use it against her interests. She trusted him and he used the information in a way that injured her financially. The issue comes down to whether we are *obligated* not to act on information someone carelessly gives us. It may be tempting to say yes, but it is not reasonable. Whatever we wish Barker had done, or conclude he should have done, we cannot make the case on the basis of obligation.

What *ideals* are involved? The obvious one is fairness. The action most in keeping with this ideal would be for Barker to have refused to take advantage of his knowledge about the house, to have considered it sold to Horace and not interfere. At the very least, if he felt impelled to outbid Horace, he could have approached the owner in such a way that the broker's commission would be paid. After all, without her help, however inadvertently it was given, he would not have known about the property.

The *consequences* (on others) of Barker's action are plain enough. The broker lost the commission. Horace and his family lost the house they almost bought.

ANALYSIS 3: POSSIBLE COURSES OF ACTION

Unless the house Horace was planning to buy was the only available house in town, Barker did have an alternative to outbidding Horace. He could have asked the broker who mentioned the house to him and his wife, or some other broker, to show them other houses.

ANALYSIS 4: THE MOST ETHICAL ACTION

In light of your analysis you would undoubtedly conclude that the three criteria—obligations, ideals, and consequences—are not of equal force. There is no real obligation involved. The consequences, though unfortunate, are not in themselves sufficiently harmful to make the action wrong. Yet Barker's action is morally wrong because it violates the ideal of fairness.

In each of the preceding cases, and in all the cases you encounter, the moral action is the action that most fully honors the obligations, ideals, and consequences involved, the action that best *fits the situation.* It is the action that *ought* to be chosen not just by the person in the case in question, but by *anyone in the same circumstances.* As subsequent chapters will reveal, the solutions to moral problems are seldom perfect solutions; they are only the best choices from among the imperfect solutions that are available.

□ A CAUTION ABOUT GENERALIZING

The temptation to move beyond the criteria we have been discussing and to develop a set of firm generalizations or "rules" of ethics is a common temptation. Although it arises from a very legitimate desire to simplify and streamline the process of analysis, it usually causes many more problems than it solves and is best avoided.*

Let's say we are analyzing a situation in which someone has taken something belonging to someone else. If we begin by applying an unqualified general rule, such as "It is wrong to take what does not belong to us," *we will have already judged the situation in question.* After making such a judgment, any analysis we do is likely to be little more than a listing of the reasons to support our predetermined conclusion. Like the juror who makes up his mind that the defendant is guilty the moment he sees him, we may appear to be weighing the evidence and may even believe that we are. Yet, in fact, we will have already made up our minds.

---

* It is possible to construct ethical rules that are so carefully shaped and qualified as to withstand even the most subtle objections. But that kind of construction is an activity that only the most advanced students of ethics should undertake. The safest and most profitable focus is on individual cases, not on generalizations.

But, someone might object, what is wrong in starting with a rule like "It's wrong to take something that does not belong to us"? Doesn't such a generalization fit most cases? Certainly, and that is just the problem. The generalization about the wrongness of taking what doesn't belong to us would cover numerous situations from bank robbery to embezzlement to stealing hubcaps and even to pocketing the extra change the supermarket cashier gave us by mistake. But it doesn't cover the exceptions, such as finding some change in a public telephone booth or taking in a stray dog and (after advertising in the local paper and not finding the owner) keeping it. In judging any particular case we must be concerned with precisely that: *whether there is anything about the case that makes it the exception to the rule.*

It is tempting to protest that there must be some generalization that applies in all cases. "Do unto others as you would have them do unto you" comes to mind. What, after all, is more basic to morality than this Golden Rule found in virtually all advanced moral systems? And yet, as Paul A. Freund has pointed out, even this rule has its exception, for a masochist's application of it would prompt him to torture others.

An interesting illustration of the danger of relying on sweeping ethical generalizations and the importance of inquiring into the circumstances of the case occurred some years ago. In Willowbrook State Hospital, an institution for the retarded, medical doctors intentionally infected entering children with an infectious hepatitis virus. On first consideration, such behavior seems outrageous. It calls to mind the barbarisms of Nazi concentration camps. In fact, not a few critics regarded the action as precisely such a moral atrocity.

The details of the situation, however, undermine that judgment. It was known that a mild form of hepatitis was rife in the institution. Historical data showed that most of the newly admitted children would be infected by natural means. By deliberately infecting newly admitted patients, the doctors could assure them a milder case of the disease, and they could be given special housing and care while ill. Moreover, the plan had been reviewed and approved by several agencies, and parental consent was obtained before a child was infected.[2]

The tendency to respond to issues with unqualified generalizations, though natural enough, should not be indulged. The people we are writing for or speaking with deserve better from us. Every important ethical issue demands our careful attention, not only to its similarity to other issues, but also to its dissimilarity, to its uniqueness. To give less, to merely mouth an overall, ready-made response is not to use moral rules, but to be used by them; not to be guided by our experience, but to be controlled by it. It takes wisdom to know when the case at hand fits the rule and when it is the exception to it. Such wisdom does not come easily. And if we substitute generalization for analysis, it does not come at all.

□ AVOIDING OTHER ERRORS

In addition to overgeneralization, four other errors are common in the analysis of moral issues: double standard, unwarranted assumptions, oversimplifications, and hasty conclusions. We will examine each in turn.

DOUBLE STANDARD

The error of the *double standard* consists of using one set of criteria for judging cases that concern us or someone we identify with and another set for judging other cases. It involves viewing evidence selectively or twisting it to serve our own interests. It is especially common in cases where we have a strong commitment to a certain action, often because we have chosen it ourselves in similar cases and wish to avoid self-condemnation.

For example, we may judge most cases of taking what does not belong to one according to the criteria of obligations, ideals, and consequences. However, when we encounter a case that comes close to home— let's say, taking clothes from a roommate or taking money from a parent without permission—we tend to set aside the criteria and construct irrational arguments or rationalizations to justify the action. Such lapses are understandable but not justifiable. Similar cases should be judged similarly. The fact that a case involves us in some way should make no difference.

To find the error of the double standard in your moral reasoning, be alert for situations in which you have a personal emotional stake. When you encounter such situations, ask yourself whether you have applied the criteria consistently, as you would in any other case. Look for signs that you have slipped into special pleading.

UNWARRANTED ASSUMPTIONS

The error of *unwarranted assumptions* consists of taking too much for granted. The fact that it usually occurs unconsciously makes it a particularly troublesome error. We usually make unwarranted assumptions whenever we read a case carelessly and fail to distinguish between what it says and what it does not say; in other words, when we read into the case details that are not there. Take, for example, the case of Agatha's relationship, which we discussed earlier in this chapter. The fact that Agatha has been seeing her minister frequently may lead some people to assume that her husband is guilty of neglecting her. That assumption is not warranted because the statement of the case neither directly nor indirectly suggests such a condition.

To avoid unwarranted assumptions, read the statement of every case carefully. Note what is said. As suggested earlier, raise important questions about the case and speculate about possible answers. Then address each significant possibility with "If . . . then" reasoning. To say, "If Agatha had a serious problem in her relationship with her husband and because of that problem sought fulfillment through her friendship with the minister, then . . ." is a legitimate approach to solving the problem. But to assume the condition to be so, without sufficient justification to warrant that assumption, is not legitimate.

OVERSIMPLIFICATIONS

It is natural enough to want to simplify matters. It is often necessary to do so to make sense of cases and to communicate our judgment to others. Simplification is not objectionable; it is *over*simplification that is an error. *Oversimplification* exists whenever our treatment of a case goes beyond reducing it to manageable proportions and *distorts* it. In moral reasoning, oversimplification is usually caused by omitting consideration of some important criterion—an obligation, for example, or a significant consequence. In the case of Agatha's relationship, if our analysis ignored the impact of the relationship on Agatha's children or the possible consequences on the minister's work, we would be guilty of oversimplifying the issue.

To avoid oversimplification, be thorough in your identification of the relevant criteria. Do not be satisfied with acknowledging the most obvious ones; consider all of them. In addition, be prepared for complexity and address it carefully when you find it.

HASTY CONCLUSIONS

Drawing *hasty conclusions* refers to embracing a judgment before we have examined the case fully. Sometimes it results from lack of time to do a thorough analysis. More often, however, it results from accepting first impressions uncritically or from approaching the case with a preconceived notion of what the solution will be. Such impressions and preconceived notions are natural enough. Whenever we encounter a case, our mind begins making associations with thousands of experiences. More quickly than the fastest computer, it identifies the experiences that are analogous and presents to us the conclusions we have reached for those cases or have decided to apply to all such cases. The problem is that those conclusions may not really fit the case in question.

To avoid making a hasty conclusion, make *no* conclusion until you have completed your analysis of the issue. Whenever a possibility occurs to you, write it down for later consideration. But resist the temptation to embrace any conclusion immediately, even if, at first thought, it seems unassailable.

Being familiar with the errors discussed here and using the strategies suggested for avoiding them will help you keep your moral reasoning sound. There is, however, one additional approach you can take: Think of yourself as two people, an *idea producer* and an *idea evaluator.* Let the first "you" generate as many varied ideas as it wishes, but before accepting them or presenting them to others in speaking or in writing, submit them to the scrutiny of the second "you." This approach will help you form the habit of going beyond mere thinking to *thinking about thinking.* That is the habit of the philosopher.

▣ INQUIRIES

1. Review your responses to the ethical issues in Chapter 6, inquiry 4. Decide which responses should be modified or expanded in light of what you have learned in this chapter. Identify those responses and explain your changes.

2. *Consumer Reports* magazine examined the growing practice of advertising in and around schools. The school buses that transport many children to school are decorated with advertisements, as are the hallways and restrooms. School corridors and cafeterias pipe in popular music punctuated by commercials. Workbooks, instructional videos, and other classroom materials contain messages from sponsors. For example, the National Live Stock and Meat Board claims that meat consumption makes people taller, and Proctor and Gamble suggests that clear-cut logging (the equivalent of strip mining) is beneficial to the environment. More significantly, Channel One, a daily news broadcast, is mandatory in many school systems. Roughly two students out of every five enrolled in U.S. schools watch Channel One, which consists of ten minutes of news and two minutes of commercials for Snickers, Rold Gold pretzels, CareFree bubble gum, Pepsi, and Reebok shoes, among other products. Advertisers pay the schools substantial fees, which can be used to purchase school supplies and equipment.[3] Apply the ethical criteria presented in this chapter and decide whether such advertising practices are morally defensible.

3. Apply what you have learned in this chapter to the following questions. Explain your answers:

a. Is it morally permissible to drive a car after having one drink? Two? Three? After how many drinks would it be wrong to drive a car? After how many drinks would it be wrong for an airline pilot to fly a commercial airplane?

b. Is it ethical to take habit-forming drugs? Is it ethical to use a substance for which the research evidence is not yet conclusive and which might be harmful?

c. Is it wrong for people to starve themselves as a means of political protest?

d. Is it ethical for the United States to sell weapons to other countries?

e. Do people who take the lives of others have any moral responsibility to their victims' families? (For example, are they obligated to provide financial assistance to the families?) Would a case of accidental death be different from a case of murder?

Evaluate the action in each of the following cases, applying what you learned in this chapter and explaining your reasoning carefully.

4. Claude challenges the principle of respect for persons with the following argument: "Past ages were simpler. Our grandparents knew personally the people they had contact with every day. Yet today the world has grown impersonal. We deal with telephone operators, airline personnel, cab drivers, people at the other end of computer lines. We don't know them and they don't know us. So the idea of respect for persons no longer holds." Construct a reply to Claude's argument.

5. The science of genetic testing is fast reaching the point where it can be determined whether people carry genes for crippling, often fatal diseases. Before long, employers will be able to know in advance whether job candidates are likely to need time off for illness; they can reject such candidates in advance. Further, health insurance companies may deny policies to such individuals. They may even refuse to reimburse parents for the delivery of a child known to be disabled before birth.

6. A seventh-grade teacher divides his class into teams to research some history topics and report to the class. Each team consists of four students. One team presents a report that is excellent in substance. However, two members of the team behave childishly while making their contributions, so the overall presentation is flawed. The teacher lowers the team's mark a full letter grade. Since the grade recorded for each team member is identical to the team grade, each member is penalized.

7. A businessman is waiting for an elevator in his office building. A stranger motions him aside and whispers, "Wanna buy a fur coat for your wife? Two hundred dollars. No questions asked. What say?" He opens a large paper bag to reveal the coat. The businessman looks at it, touches it, and realizes that the coat is unquestionably mink and worth at least ten times what the man is asking for it. He takes out his wallet, hands over the $200, and takes the bag.

8. A common method for dispatching animals in slaughterhouses is to hit them on the head with a sledgehammer as many times as necessary to drive them into semiconsciousness, then to impale one of their rear legs, hoist them into the air, and slit their throats, leaving them to bleed to death.

9. A woman learns that her son-in-law fathered an illegitimate child several years before he met her daughter. (He and his wife have been happily married for ten years. They are childless.) She is sure her daughter is not aware of this and has reason to doubt that she would ever find out about it by herself. The woman feels obliged to tell her, however, and does so.

10. The executives of a large company are planning their advertising campaign for the coming year. They would prefer to use a simple and honest approach, but they know that their competitors use devious psychological approaches and even outright lies in their advertising. The executives fear that if they do not use the same approaches as their competitors, their company's profits will suffer and they may lose their jobs. They decide to play it safe and use those approaches.

11. A man and woman, both college students, have been living together off campus for three years. They have never considered marrying, and it has always been implicit in their relationship that each should be free to leave the other any time he or she wishes. Unexpectedly, the woman becomes pregnant. Since she is opposed to abortion, she resigns herself to having the child. When she is seven months pregnant, the man decides to leave her. One day when she is out shopping for groceries, he gathers his belongings, scribbles a hasty note ("Our relationship was beautiful while it lasted, but it's over"), and leaves.

12. A businessman wishes to invest some money in wooded land. He knows that he can sell the trees for lumber, plant more trees, and sell them when they mature. He will be serving the cause of ecology at the same time he makes a modest income. After finding a parcel of land that is appropriate for his purposes, he asks the owner the selling price. The price is so ridiculously low that the man realizes the owner is unaware of the value of the trees as lumber. He ponders whether it is immoral to buy the land at such a price. He decides it is not and buys it.

13. A young woman has a serious kidney disease. She undergoes expensive care while awaiting the availability of a donor's kidney. One day she receives word that a donor has been found. She looks forward happily to the transplant operation. Then she finds out that the donor is an institutionalized mental defective who is unable to understand the nature of the operation and the remote possible danger to him should his other kidney ever become damaged. The surgeon will be removing the organ without his permission. The young woman accepts the kidney anyway.

14. Knowing that after negotiations with management are completed they will get less than they ask for in wages and fringe benefits, some labor unions begin negotiations by demanding more than is reasonable.

15. Allegedly, the U.S. Army has researched mechanical ways to control human behavior. For example, they conducted experiments with devices that used "flickering light of varying intensity" to render the brain incapable of controlling the body and with devices that emit inaudible sound to confuse the mind and cause pain. (An army spokesman stated that such devices might be useful in controlling crowds.)[4]

16. A newspaper carrier begins his job with enthusiasm. His supervisor explains that once or twice a week, advertising inserts will be delivered with the papers and must be placed inside them. The job of insertion is a time-consuming chore, the supervisor explains, and paper carriers are easily tempted to discard the inserts. However, the supervisor warns, discarding them is grounds for dismissal, because the advertisers pay for them and have a right to expect them to reach the customers. Not only is each newspaper carrier expected to handle his or her own inserts properly, the carrier is also expected to report any other paper carrier who does not do so. Two weeks later, the boy notices that all the other delivery people in his town regularly throw the inserts in a trash barrel. He reports them to his supervisor.

17. Midwestern University is a national football power. The alumni association, which exerts considerable influence on the university's affairs, does not tolerate losing teams or any faculty member or administrator who stands in the way of victory. This year Professor Woebegone has had the misfortune of having Roger Rapid, star halfback, in his mathematics class. Roger is mathematically illiterate. After spending many extra hours with Roger in hopes of dragging him through the course successfully, Professor Woebegone has been forced to admit failure. On the final exam Roger has scored 27. Judged by the grading scale in the course, his final average is an F. Since he is a borderline student in other courses, an F will place him on academic probation, and he will be ineligible for the last crucial game of the season. Without him the team will surely lose the conference title. Professor Woebegone, who is untenured, may well lose his job. The professor turns in a D+ grade for Roger.

18. A businesswoman realizes that with the local college enrollment burgeoning, an investment in a trailer court will be profitable. It happens, too, that a perfect site is available. The one complication is that the owner of the land, who lives across the highway, would not sell it if he knew it would be put to such use. The businesswoman therefore pays a young married couple to buy it for her. They approach the owner, explain that they want the land to build a home on, and even show him fake building plans. After he sells the land to them, they turn it over to the businesswoman.

19. Residents of a poor neighborhood are plagued with a drug problem. Five pushers operate openly on their streets and brazenly try to entice their children to take "free samples." A committee of residents has approached the police and begged them to arrest the pushers, but they have done nothing. There is reason to believe some of the police are sharing in the proceeds of the drug trade. The residents decide that their only hope for a safe and decent neighborhood for their children is to take the law into their own hands. Accordingly, one calm summer night they unceremoniously execute the five pushers.

20. A nurse in a nursing home dispenses medication to elderly patients. The home is understaffed and, though the existing staff is efficient, there is such a demand on their time that they have difficulty in doing a quality job. The nursing supervisor frequently orders the nurse to give the patients unprescribed tranquilizers to keep them quiet and docile. This allows the staff to attend to critical needs.

21. A large grocery chain orders its personnel department to screen out all grocery clerk applicants who have a prison record, a history of alcohol/drug abuse or mental illness, or a problem with obesity.

CHAPTER EIGHT

CONSIDERING OBLIGATIONS

What do we do in situations where there is more than a single obligation? How can we reconcile conflicting obligations?

The numerous obligations noted in the previous chapter are classified as obligations of *fidelity* (faithfulness) and are characterized by an actual or implied promise to others. There are, however, other kinds of obligations; British ethicist W. D. Ross identified the following ones:

Obligations of reparation: These obligations require us to make amends for the wrongs we commit by removing, to whatever extent we can, the harmful consequences caused by those wrongs.

Obligations of gratitude: These obligations require us to demonstrate our appreciation for the considerateness others have shown us. When we express gratitude in words or deeds, we are not merely extending a courtesy to others but are fulfilling a debt that their kindness has created for us.

Obligations of self-improvement: These obligations, Ross argues, arise simply from the potential each of us has for improvement in virtue or (moral) intelligence.

Obligations of justice: Obligations of justice demand that we give each person equal consideration. This does not mean that everyone must be treated exactly alike; it means that everyone must be given his or her due and that no partiality be shown to anyone's interests (including our own). Accordingly, differences in treatment should be in proportion to differences in what the facts show each person deserves.

Obligations of beneficence: These obligations require us to do good acts for their own sake; that is, for no other reason than that they are good.

Obligations of non-maleficence: These obligations require us to avoid doing injury to others. At first consideration, such obligations may seem to be merely the negative corollary to obligations of beneficence. But Ross argues that they are a distinct category; moreover, he argues that obligations of non-maleficence are even *more* binding than those of beneficence. He reasons that "we should not in general consider it justifiable to kill one person in order to keep another alive, or to steal from one in order to give alms to another."[1]

Taken together, obligations of beneficence and non-maleficence are a logical extension of an idea that is fundamental to all ethical systems—that morality consists of both avoiding evil and doing good. This idea, it could be argued, is (like the principle of right desire) *self-evident* since evil is by definition something to be avoided and good is by definition something to be prized.

□ WHEN OBLIGATIONS CONFLICT

Any one of these obligations may be present by itself in a moral situation. But more often two or more are present; and many times they conflict. In such cases the problem is to choose wisely among them.

The executives of a corporation, for example, must make a difficult decision. Their profit picture has been dismal. If they do not find some way to cut back their expenses, they may be driven into bankruptcy. Since their biggest expense is salaries, it is clear they must make economies there. After analyzing the various operations of the corporation, they determine that they can effect significant economies by curtailing certain services to customers and combining the work of three departments.

This reorganization will make it possible to reduce the work staff by twelve people and result in savings of tens of thousands of dollars. However, each of the people involved has been employed by the company for more than fifteen years, and all are between ages 45 and 55. They are too young for retirement and too old to find other positions very easily.

The dilemma the executives face is the conflict between their obligation to long-time and faithful employees and their obligation to stockholders. Both obligations demand fulfillment. Both obviously cannot be fulfilled. There may be some middle ground possible—some special waiving of the retirement rules that will permit at least some employees to retire early. But even in cases where the executives have the power to grant such a waiver, it is unlikely that they could do it for all twelve people. Choice is unavoidable. They must give preference to one obligation or the other.

Another very common example of a moral dilemma caused by conflicting obligations is that faced by the person who is asked to give a job reference for a colleague or subordinate whom he or she believes may not be able to perform the job in question. The chairman of an academic department, for instance, may be called by his counterpart in another school. "I'm calling about an applicant of ours who worked for you until last year," the caller says. "His name is Dr. Elmo Ryan, and he's applying for a position in sociology." The chairman winces. He remembers Ryan all too well. For three years the poor man struggled to teach his courses well. The chairman visited his classes and tried to help him improve. Several of his colleagues in the department did likewise. Finally, everyone was driven to the same conclusion that the students who were unfortunate enough to be in his classes had long since reached: Ryan simply was not meant to be a teacher.

Now the chairman must answer a direct question about him to a prospective employer. If he tells her the truth about Ryan—that he is a hardworking, personable, cooperative *incompetent*—Ryan will surely lose the job. The chairman feels a certain obligation to Ryan. And yet he feels obligated to the woman on the phone and to all the students Ryan might be assigned to teach. Whatever the chairman decides to do, the decision will not be easy. It will require breaking one obligation.

Does everyone have an obligation to assist in the rehabilitation of former thieves and rapists by giving them a chance to return to society without discrimination? Most of us would agree that there is such an obligation, at least one of beneficence. But if a banker wants to honor that obligation and hire the reformed thief, he or she must also consider the obligation to his or her customers and to the Federal Deposit Insurance Corporation to maintain the security of the bank. If the owners of a girls' camp wish to honor that obligation and hire the reformed rapist, they must consider their obligation to ensure the safety of their clientele.

□ WEIGHING THE OBLIGATIONS

In cases where two or more obligations are in conflict, the best we can do is to *consider the relative importance of each and give preference to the more important one.* Of course, which obligation is more important is often a decision about which honest, intelligent people may disagree. To judge well we need a sense of proportion. That is, we need to perceive what balance among the obligations will serve each one to the extent appropriate and thereby make the best of a difficult situation. Whenever both obligations can be partly served, they should be. Whenever only one can be served, the more important one should be.

If a person owes $200 to someone who needs the money, and then, just when he is able to pay, he reads in the paper that contributions are being sought for flood relief in a neighboring state, he may be torn between settling his debt and donating to the flood victims. Which should he do? A rationale could be developed to support either. But a better case could be made for settling his debt, not only because it existed prior to the other, but also because the creditor is in need. The obligation of justice in this case would be more important than the obligation of beneficence. (It is not necessarily so in every case where two obligations conflict. If the creditor did not need the money immediately and the act of charity were to a family that had no income and neither qualified for public assistance nor was likely to find any other private benefactor, beneficence might be more important.)

A merchandiser for a clothing concern is in her busiest season of the year. Moreover, the demands of her job this year are even greater than usual because two very different and daring fashion trends are competing with a well-entrenched mode. The right judgment on the merchandiser's part in assessing the buying public's taste will make a great deal of money for her company; the wrong judgment could ruin the company. Meanwhile her husband, whom she loves, is in a state of depression. He feels he has disappointed her by losing his job, he suspects her (wrongly) of infidelity, and he is given to periods of depression in which he contemplates suicide. The psychiatrist he has been visiting says he is not dangerously ill, but could easily become so. He advises the merchandiser to take her husband on a month's vacation.

What should the wife do? She owes her employer her expert judgment during the next month. Yet she owes her husband help and attention. Which obligation is greater? Most ethicists would undoubtedly rule in favor of the husband for two reasons: first, because the wife's obligation to him derives from a solemn vow to care for him ("in sickness and in health"); second, because his condition may be a matter of life and death.

To the extent possible she should, of course, try to serve both obligations. She might, in other words, postpone the vacation for a week or ten days and during that period work a sixteen- or eighteen-hour day. She might even take work with her on the vacation or telephone the office every day to provide whatever guidance she can to her employer. Nevertheless, it would be a graver fault to neglect her husband's needs than to neglect her employer's.

□ TWO MORAL DILEMMAS

Such choices challenge lawyers and doctors virtually every day. Clarence Darrow, the famous attorney, is said to have won a case by stealing the jury's attention during the prosecutor's summation. He smoked a cigar in which he had placed a wire to prevent the ashes from falling. With each puff the ashes would grow longer . . . and the jury would sit a little farther forward on their chairs. When would those ashes fall? They never did. However brilliant the prosecutor's closing words were, they were ineffective. The jury was too busy watching that cigar to pay any attention to them.

Darrow's bit of vaudeville represented a choice between his obligation to his client and his obligation to courtroom procedure. Obviously, in his judgment no trick was too cheap to play if it helped his client. Was his action morally blameless? Hardly. It was an open and shut case of wrongdoing, though one that we would probably be inclined to approve if our life were in the balance.

A similar case of a lawyer forced to choose between obligations occurred more recently in New York City. Martin Erdmann, a Legal Aid defender, remarked publicly that judgeships today must either be bought or won through political influence. He was brought before the New York City Bar Association for violating the group's code of ethics. (The association recommended that no action be taken against him.) Erdmann had an obligation to the legal profession to protect it from scandal, and he had an obligation to that profession, and to the citizens it represents, to speak out against abuses within the profession. Undoubtedly he judged the latter obligation to be more important.

How do we judge his action? To judge fairly we would have to know more than the details given here or available in the news accounts of his case. If the situation concerning the selection of judges is as he described it, then it makes a mockery of our system of jurisprudence and of the very concept of justice. It cries out for denunciation. His obligation to speak out would indeed take precedence over his obligation to protect his profession. On the other hand, if the situation is not as he described it, or if he wasn't sure and didn't bother to determine the validity of the description, then the obligation to be silent and not scandalize the courts would take precedence. If he had knowledge of some abuses but did not know how widespread they were, the requirement of proportion would have demanded that he modify his statement to reflect his degree of knowledge rather than speak in general terms and indict, by implication, all judges.

□ THE ALABAMA SYPHILIS CASE

In the summer of 1972 a shocking disclosure was made about a government-sponsored medical experiment that had gone on, unnoticed, for *forty years*. The experiment concerned the effects of syphilis. The Public Health Service had begun the experiment in Alabama. Its purpose was to determine the extent of the damage that syphilis will do if left untreated. (Its effects, most of them known or at least surmised at the time the experiment was begun, are blindness; deafness; degeneration of the heart, bones, and central nervous system; insanity; and death.) Six hundred black men were selected for the experiment. They were promised free transportation to the hospital, free medical treatment for diseases other than syphilis, and free burial. Apparently they did not receive clear explanations of the possible harm the disease could cause them if left untreated.

Of the six hundred, a third never developed syphilis. Half of those who did received the arsenic-mercury treatment that was standard before the discovery of penicillin. The remaining two hundred got no medication. Even after the discovery of penicillin a decade later and its widespread use as a cure for syphilis, they received no treatment. They remained human guinea pigs.

There were several obligations the researchers should have weighed. First, there was their obligation as physicians to care for their patients. Second, there was their obligation to justice, to respect other human beings and treat them in a manner consistent with their humanity. Finally, there was their obligation as researchers to serve mankind by seeking cures for deadly diseases. The researchers seem to have ignored the first two obligations completely. Apparently they thought of the men not as patients, but as the "subjects" of the experiment—as phenomena to be studied rather than as persons to be cured. If they recognized the inhumanity of their handling of the two hundred men, they failed to act upon their recognition. (There is a bitter irony in this case. During the very period in which the experiment was conducted, Nazi doctors performed similar barbarities on the inmates of concentration camps. After World War II, at the Nuremberg trials, the United States and its allies condemned those doctors for "crimes against humanity.")

The shock felt by every sensitive person at this disclosure reveals the importance of choosing well among conflicting moral obligations. It was not wrong for the doctors in the Alabama case to honor their obligation as researchers. What was wrong was their ignoring the two other obligations, both of which were more important.

□ THOROUGHNESS IS IMPORTANT

It is difficult enough to reach wise decisions in cases with conflicting obligations when we have identified all the obligations. To judge wisely when we have overlooked one or more obligations is impossible; our analysis is bound to be oversimplified. For this reason it is important to consider all possible obligations—including those of reparation, gratitude, justice, and beneficence, as well as those of fidelity—before attempting to judge.

▣ INQUIRIES

1. Review the code of ethics you examined for inquiry 2 in Chapter 6. Referring to the discussion of the types of moral obligations at the beginning of this chapter, classify each moral prescription in that code of ethics.

2. James Q. Wilson argues that "a moral life is perfected by practice more than by precept" and that social institutions, notably the family, have the power to encourage that practice and create the climate in which it takes place.[2] Would it be correct to say that the family has a moral obligation to use this power? If so, do other social agencies—for example, school, church, entertainment and communications media, government—have a similar obligation? Explain.

3. Do rich people, by virtue of their wealth, have any special ethical obligation? Why or why not?

4. Do geniuses, by virtue of their intellectual gifts, have any special ethical obligation?

Directions for inquiries 5–23: In each case, identify the conflicting obligations and decide whether the action taken is morally right. Be sure to consider the requirement of proportion.

5. Rhoda enjoys socializing with fellow employees at work, but their discussion usually consists of gossiping about other people, including several of her friends. At first Rhoda feels uncomfortable talking in this way about people she is close to, but then she decides it does no real harm and so she feels no remorse for joining in.

6. When 2 Live Crew's album, *As Nasty as They Want to Be,* was judged obscene and banned in Florida, Roger reacted as many people did. He denounced the decision loudly and often to his friends and business associates. He even wrote a letter to his local newspaper warning of the dangers of censorship and branding the album's critics as "blue-nosed, puritanical know-nothings." When his wife asked him if he had heard the album or read the lyrics of its songs, he admitted that he hadn't, adding that he didn't have to be familiar with the lyrics to know that they shouldn't be censored.

7. In studying the subculture of a particular group, a sociologist must be accepted by the people and gain their trust. One such researcher is studying the people in an urban slum. She learns through their confidence that certain members of the community are involved in a car-theft ring. She does not report them to the police.

8. A Roman Catholic priest disagrees with his church on the issue of abortion. A parishioner comes to him for guidance. He does not mention the Church's official position on the subject, but gives her his own moral judgment.

9. An executive of a large company learns that the company is violating the state antipollution law by dumping chemicals into the lake bordering its plant. The state inspectors are being bribed to ignore the violation. The executive takes no action.

10. A professor of psychology wishes to learn the effects of various conditions on students' learning. He significantly varies the heat, lighting, noise, and humidity of his classroom during examinations. On occasion he also purposely garbles half a lecture or repeats a previous day's lecture verbatim without comment.

11. A senator believes strongly that the country has oversubscribed the defense program to the detriment of social services. Yet he is from a state that receives a large number of defense contracts, and if he introduces legislation to curtail defense spending, he is likely to be defeated in the next election. He decides not to introduce it.

12. A very competent druggist, well-versed in the latest pharmacological studies, receives a prescription from a physician and recognizes that it is for a dangerous, highly addictive, and largely discredited medication. She calls the physician and is told curtly to mind her own business. As the customer waits in the front of the store, the druggist ponders the situation. "Should I refuse to fill it? Should I tell the customer I am certain the doctor has made a mistake? Should I call the medical board and report the incident?" She decides to fill the prescription.

13. An Old Testament professor in a Protestant seminary does not accept the school's literal interpretation of the Bible. In his classes he introduces his students to a number of philosophies of interpretation, including liberal ones. Learning of this violation of the school's traditional theological perspective, the faculty deliberates about it at length. Finally they reach a decision. The professor is to be fired.

14. Vincent LoDato, a California theoretical physicist, completed his calculations concerning means of controlling thermonuclear fusion. He applied for an $80,000 grant from the Atomic Energy Commission to have his equations computer-examined. After reviewing his calculations, the commission decided that they involved processes useful in controlled nuclear fusion and related to the making of hydrogen bombs. The commission therefore stamped every page of his notebook "secret/classified," forced him to withdraw a scientific report he had submitted to a journal for publication, and ordered him to cease working on the subject in question. In LoDato's judgment, the commission forced him out of that area of research.[3]

15. A doctor on duty in a hospital emergency room one Halloween night treats a 15-year-old boy whose eye was injured by an exploding firecracker. He notices the boy is drunk. Because the extent of the injury is not certain, he has the boy admitted to the hospital and notifies his parents. When they arrive, the boy is under sedation, so his drunken condition escapes their detection. Nevertheless, the doctor informs them that their son had been drinking.

16. A psychiatrist is treating a very disturbed and potentially violent man. One day the man tells her that he has recurring thoughts of killing a stranger, whom he will choose at random. He details exactly how he will carry out the crime. A few days later the psychiatrist reads in the newspaper that the very same crime her patient described has been committed. She has no doubt that her patient committed it; every detail is identical. The psychiatrist would like to inform the police, but she decides not to.

17. A hijacker is holding a jetliner and 192 passengers hostage until his demands are met. He is demanding $500,000 and a guarantee of safe passage to a country that will not return him for prosecution. The airline authorities and the police agree to his demands, and he releases the plane and the hostages. Then the police seize him and take him to jail.

18. A company president receives an angry letter from a high government official. It seems an executive of the company has written a letter to a large daily newspaper criticizing the official's policy decisions. (She wrote as a private citizen, not as a representative of her company.) The government official is demanding that the executive be fired. If she is not, he warns, the company will lose some lucrative government contracts. The president ponders the matter and decides to fire the executive.

19. When Sally's father was gravely ill, he called her to his bedside and said, "I'd always hoped I'd see you graduate from college and go on to become a physicist, but I know death is near. Promise me one thing—that you'll keep on studying hard and become a physicist." Sally was deeply moved. "I will," she responded; "I swear to you I will." Her father died shortly thereafter. Now it is two years later, and Sally is ready to graduate from college. But she will not become a physicist. She has decided to go to law school.

20. A restaurant cook is working a busy dinner shift on Friday night. In his hurry, he drops two expensive cooked steaks on the floor. He picks the steaks up, puts them on two platters, and calls for them to be served.

21. A carpenter with a wife and three children works for a home construction firm that is barely able to make its payroll. The current job is for ten houses in a new development. The carpenter is aware that the lumber for the inside walls is inferior to the grade required in the architect's specifications; eventually, the walls could warp. However, he does the job as he is told and says nothing.

22. Portia is a legal secretary hired with the understanding that all office information will be confidential. Her boss, a criminal lawyer in a large city, defends a man accused of vicious attacks on several elderly women. In the course of her work, Portia learns that the accused has told her boss that he committed the crimes and feels no remorse. A plea of "not guilty" is being entered and there is a good chance the man will serve no time for his crimes. What, if anything, should Portia do?

23. Claude, a college freshman, learns that his roommate and friend is pushing hard drugs on campus. Claude is not opposed to drug use. He smokes marijuana himself, though he has never used any hard drugs. Neither does he believe that drug pushing is wrong. But he does fear for his own safety, since if his friend is discovered and their room searched, his own marijuana might be found. After removing his marijuana from his room, he slips an anonymous note under the dean's door, informing on his roommate.

⌐ CHAPTER NINE ¬

CONSIDERING IDEALS

*How can we reconcile conflicts between ideals or
between an ideal and an obligation?*

In some contemporary contexts the word *ideal* has acquired the connota-
tion of impracticality. Thus, we may say something is ideal when we
really mean unrealistic; we may call people idealistic when they produce
grand but unworkable ideas. From that perspective, having and valuing
ideals understandably seems naive and even foolish. Yet there is nothing
impractical or unrealistic about the term *ideal* as it is used in ethical analysis. As noted in Chapter 7, to an ethicist ideals are not only notions of
excellence, goals that bring greater harmony in ourselves and with others,
but they are also specific concepts that assist us in achieving respect for
persons in our judgments and actions. Among the ideals that figure
prominently in ethical reasoning, we saw, are fairness, tolerance, compassion, loyalty, forgiveness, amity, and peace. Other important ideals are
truthfulness, honesty, integrity, social responsibility, and the four cardinal
virtues conceptualized by the ancient Greeks. The cardinal virtues are as
follows:

> *Prudence.* This virtue, known also as "practical wisdom," consists of
> choosing one's behavior judiciously by consulting experience and
> deliberating thoughtfully about what response is most appropriate.
> Prudence is the exact opposite of rashness and impulsiveness.

Justice. Justice denotes the evaluation of situations according to their merits, without prejudice, and giving each person his or her due. This virtue is the cornerstone of law.

Temperance. Socrates considered temperance to be almost synonymous with self-mastery. The temperate person, he argued, is the one who exercises control over his or her desires and thereby escapes domination by them. Aristotle took a similar view, holding self-indulgence to be childish. For these philosophers, and for many of the ethicists that followed them, the hallmarks of temperance are moderation and restraint of one's desires and passions.[1]

Courage. This virtue "does not consist only in conquering fear and in withholding the body from flight no matter what the risk of pain. It consists at least as much in steeling the will, reinforcing its resolutions, and turning the mind relentlessly to seek or face the truth."[2] Courage thus has an intellectual and a moral, as well as a physical, dimension.

To the cardinal virtues Christian philosophers added the theological virtues of faith, hope, and charity. Today the term *charity* is most closely associated with giving material goods to the poor, but that is very different from its historical meaning. The term derives from the Latin word *caritas*, which means affection; in Christian ethics it means love—specifically, the love of God and one's neighbor. Although all three of these virtues are important components of religion-based ethics, only the third, charity, is widely accepted in philosophy-based ethics.

□ IDEALS IN PROFESSIONAL ETHICS CODES

Although popular culture often treats ideals and virtues casually and even contemptuously, they continue to be honored in the ethical codes of professional organizations, as the following examples illustrate:[3]

TRUTHFULNESS

"Engineers shall issue public statements only in an objective and truthful manner." *American Society of Mechanical Engineers*

HONESTY

"It is the duty of the chemist . . . to be diligent in exposing and opposing such errors and frauds as the chemist's special knowledge brings to light." *American Institute of Chemists, Inc.*

"Whenever necessary to avoid misleading [others], psychologists acknowledge the limits of their data or conclusions." *American Psychological Association*

INTEGRITY

"A pharmacist acts with honesty and integrity in professional relationships." *American Pharmaceutical Association*

"Psychologists seek to promote integrity in the science, teaching, and practice of psychology." *American Psychological Association*

"Members shall act at all times with integrity and in a responsible manner." *American Society of Zoologists*

SOCIAL RESPONSIBILITY

"Psychologists are aware of their professional and scientific responsibilities to the community and the society in which they work and live." *American Psychological Association*

"Members shall use special knowledge and skills for the advancement of human welfare." *American Society of Zoologists*

FAIRNESS

"It is the duty of the chemist . . . to work and act in a strict spirit of fairness to employers, clients, contractors, and employees, and in a spirit of personal helpfulness and fraternity toward other members of the chemical profession." *American Institute of Chemists, Inc.*

"An experimental or theoretical study may sometimes justify criticism, even severe criticism, of the work of another scientist. When appropriate, such criticism may be offered in published papers. However, in no case is personal criticism considered to be appropriate." *American Chemical Society*

"[Members] will not discriminate against others on the basis of sex, sexual orientation, creed, religion, race, color, national origin, age, economic status, cultural mores, physical handicaps, or organizational affiliation." *Ecological Society of America*

PRUDENCE

"Engineers shall associate only with reputable persons or organizations." *American Society of Mechanical Engineers*

JUSTICE

"Microbiologists recognize responsibilities to students, technicians, and other associates working under their supervision to consider them colleagues, to provide training where required, and to assign appropriate recognition for their contributions." *American Society for Microbiology*

TEMPERANCE

"A scientist should not proclaim a discovery to the public unless the experimental, statistical, or theoretical support for it is of strength sufficient to warrant publication in the scientific literature." *American Chemical Society*

□ IDEALS IN CONFLICT

Ideals, like obligations, do not always harmonize with one another. In many situations they compete with one another. Consider this case. A kindergarten boy from a poor family rides the school bus to and from school. On the half-hour ride many of the other children on the bus entertain themselves by teasing him about his plain clothes, his unkempt hair, his worn shoes. Day by day the abuse continues, becoming more and more cruel. An 11-year-old girl, sensitive to the feelings of others, notices the boy suffering in silence, unable to understand why the other students want to make him feel bad. The girl is repulsed by his appearance and is not at all eager to alienate her friends. Honesty bids her stay out of the affair. But kindness prompts her to sit with him, speak with him, become a "big sister" he can look forward to seeing each day on the bus so that the rejection of the others will not scar him emotionally.

By choosing to honor the ideal of kindness, the girl necessarily violates the ideal of honesty. Does she do right? If we believe kindness to be the higher ideal in this situation, we will agree that she does.

An interesting case of conflicting ideals occurred in the filming of a documentary account of the life of a young evangelist (now a movie actor), Marjoe Gortner. The film shows how Marjoe perfected and used his pentecostal pitch on crowds of believers. He didn't believe he was preaching a "miracle of God." In fact, he didn't even believe in God! The producers intended the film to reveal this and thus to serve the ideal of honest reporting. However, in filming the revival meeting scenes they used real revival meetings that were set up by Marjoe. Thus the crowds

who appear on the screen were exploited, their religious beliefs by implication mocked in the film.[4]

Was the use of real believers in real revival meetings morally justified? To decide, we must consider whether the ideal of honesty in reporting outweighed the ideal of respect for the many sincere believers and tolerance of their beliefs. In other words, we must determine which ideal
represented the *greater good* (or the lesser evil).

If there had been no way to create a set and use actors, or perhaps if
the point of the film had never been made before, then the ideal of honesty in reporting might have taken precedence. But there was a way, and
though it would have been more expensive in time and money, the cost
would not seem to have been prohibitive. Furthermore, the point had
been made in books and films. Therefore, the offense to the people and the
insult to their beliefs outweighed the authenticity achieved. The producers' decision did not represent the greater good.

□ THE MUNICH INCIDENT

Two decades ago the world shared the dilemma of West German police
officials when Arab guerrillas held members of the Israeli Olympic team
hostage and attempted to leave the country with them. The police were
faced with the decision of how best to free the Israelis with a minimum of
harm to everyone concerned. The ideal of respect for the rights and safety
of the victims clashed with the ideal of respect for the lives of the guerrillas. If the guerrillas were allowed to leave the country with their hostages,
the hostages faced almost certain torture and death. Yet if the police tried
to prevent them from leaving, the lives of both would be threatened.

The police tried to minimize the danger by tricking the guerrillas,
gaining entry to the buildings they had taken over, and subduing them.
But after this and other efforts failed and the guerrillas and their captives
were at the airport, the police were left with their final plan—to separate
the guerrillas, kill their leader, and either overpower the others or persuade them to surrender. (The plan did not work as intended.)

Was the plan to murder the leader justified? Had it been the first
response, it surely would have been questionable. Human life, even the
life of a criminal, is a precious thing and should not be treated lightly. In
this case, however, it was a last resort, put into effect only after other less
violent actions had failed. Finally, since it was designed to save lives, it
was surely justified. The only alternative to it would have been to stand
by while many innocent people were taken to their deaths. Was it, then, a

desirable action that decent men could be proud of performing? No. But it was the lesser of two evils.

□ THE ISSUE OF AFFIRMATIVE ACTION

The debate over the wisdom of "affirmative action" has taken place mainly in the political arena. Yet the issue is essentially a moral one involving conflicting ideals—or, more precisely, conflicting expressions of a single ideal, fairness. Affirmative action was conceived as a means of overcoming the effects of centuries of discrimination. Several decades ago more and more people became convinced that denying education and employment opportunities to women merely on the basis of their gender and to black (or Hispanic) men merely on the basis of their color (or ethnicity) was unfair and therefore unethical.

Clearly, decency required that something be done to correct the situation. But what was the best and most reasonable approach? One idea was to guarantee equal educational and employment opportunity to all citizens and to create laws providing for the prosecution of individuals who failed to honor that guarantee. Critics responded that such a guarantee was fine for the future but did nothing to correct past injustices. Another idea was to provide special educational "catch-up" programs to offset academic deprivation. Critics argued that this solution would not achieve results quickly enough; the only fair solution, in their view, would be to give women and minority men *preference* over white males in college admissions and employment. Such preference generally took the form of "set-asides" and hiring quotas.

Although arguments against preferences were initially dismissed as shallow and, in some cases, racist, in recent years they have been given a more impartial hearing. One such argument is that preferences cause racial animosity; another is that they cheat the very people they are designed to help by putting them in educational or employment situations for which they have not been prepared; a third is that they deprive society of the most highly trained and qualified people. But the most common, and perhaps most substantive, argument is that preferences have resulted less in fairness toward women and minority males than in unfairness towards white males. Those who advance this argument maintain that the only fair system is one that is completely blind to gender, race, and ethnicity and judges each individual solely on his or her qualifications. However the affirmative action issue is ultimately resolved, it offers an unmistakable lesson—even when an ideal is universally accepted, it can still be very difficult to achieve.

☐ IDEALS VERSUS OBLIGATIONS

Frequently, ideals compete not with themselves, but with obligations. Every time a police officer takes a gun from a criminal, he or she is choosing the obligation to prevent crime over the ideal of respecting private property. Every time a doctor prescribes a placebo for a hypochondriac patient, he or she is placing the obligation to care for the patient over the ideal of honesty. Most people would agree with the choices made in such cases. There are situations, however, in which the promptings of ideal and obligation are more nearly balanced.

The body of a man who died from cancer has just been delivered to the funeral home. As the mortician begins to prepare the body for burial, the telephone rings. The caller is the director of a nearby medical school. It seems that the type of cancer the man had is very rare and the opportunity to study it more closely could provide valuable insights in the fight to cure cancer. The director and his staff, as well as the medical staff of the hospital, had suggested that the man will his body to the medical center, but he had refused. After his death they pleaded with the man's relatives to permit an autopsy. They refused. The purpose of his call, the director explains, is to request that the mortician cooperate with them and permit the autopsy to be made without the relatives' knowledge.

The mortician is being asked to set aside his obligation to the relatives to treat the body as they wish and instead to honor the ideal of concern for the suffering of other human beings. If the autopsy were certain to provide needed insights in the study of cancer, we might conclude that he should agree to the autopsy. Since it offers only a possibility, and since his obligation to the family is not casual, but serious and formal, the mortician should refuse.

Consider still another case. Simone's cousin comes to her house one evening and explains that he is in a desperate situation. He has been in debt to loan sharks for some time and has been able to postpone the due date several times. Now his time is up. He has received the final warning: Pay up tonight or die. He must raise $23,000 in five hours. It is futile even to try to raise the money. He could turn himself in to the police, but that would be only a temporary solution. The moment he was released from their custody, his life would again be in jeopardy. All he can hope for is to hide out for a week or ten days and then attempt to slip out of the country. He begs Simone to hide him in her home for a while.

Simone weighs the matter. She and her cousin have never been close. She hasn't even seen him in ten years. But the cousin's life is at stake. Simple charity demands that Simone honor his request. On the other hand, if Simone harbors him in her own home, he will surely be endangering her husband and children, whom she has an obligation to protect. The people who will be searching for her cousin are not likely to look kindly on witnesses who can identify them. Furthermore, they are probably not above harming women and children.

If there is any way that Simone can help her cousin without endangering herself and her loved ones, morality demands that she do so. However, for Simone to choose to help her cousin at the expense of endangering herself and her family would be a greater wrong. It is not necessary that Simone be certain that her immediate family would be harmed. The likelihood that they would be is sufficient cause for her to deny her cousin the act of charity.

In summary, then, in cases in which there is a conflict between ideals or between an ideal and an obligation, we should choose the action that will achieve the greater good. Where the choice of actions is such that no good can be achieved, we should choose the action that will result in the lesser evil.

▣ INQUIRIES

In each of the following cases, identify the ideals, or ideals and obligations, that are in conflict. Examine the action taken or proposed and decide whether it achieves the greater good (or lesser harm).

1. The world's largest cigarette company, Philip Morris, donates millions of dollars to museums, theaters, dance companies, and arts groups in New York City, where its corporate headquarters are located. When the city was about to enact tough smoking restrictions, Philip Morris reportedly contacted the various groups and let them know that future grants would be affected by the level of support they received in their fight against the city. Many of the groups joined the lobbying effort and barraged City Hall with calls and letters opposing the smoking restrictions.

Editorials in the *Chronicle of Philanthropy* and elsewhere criticized Philip Morris for its pressure tactics.[5]

2. A University of Massachusetts professor has argued that a sexual relationship between a professor and a student can be "quite beautiful and genuinely transforming" and can "touch a student in a positive way." He specifies a situation in which a female college student who had "unnaturally" prolonged her virginity offered it to her professor and the professor accepted it.[6]

3. Is patriotism a moral ideal? In other words, is it good to love one's country and its institutions and bad to hate or speak out against them? Does your answer depend on the particular country and institutions in question? Explain.

4. Trudy is an executive with a large corporation. After reading a confidential memorandum revealing that her corporation is concluding negotiations to buy several smaller companies, she realizes that an immediate investment in those companies before news of the buyout becomes public will result in a handsome profit. So she invests $10,000 of her own money and tells her family and friends to do likewise.

5. Ronald, a senior editor at a publishing house, receives a book manuscript written by a celebrity. He skims it and immediately recognizes that it is filled with details about the personal lives of dozens of prominent people. Unquestionably, it will ruin reputations and cause many people pain. On the other hand, given the public's taste for scandal, it is bound to make the best-seller list and earn his company a lot of money. He decides to offer the celebrity a contract on the book.

6. Doris, an art historian, spends much of her spare time browsing in old shops, hoping to find a valuable piece of art at a ridiculously low price. At last her perseverance has paid off. She just bought a painting worth at least $25,000 for $7.50. The shop owner obviously had no idea of its value.

7. It is a standard practice for advertising people to create ads that play on people's needs and desires. For example, they choose words and images that convey the idea that buying a certain brand of clothing will bring friendship, athletic or professional success, love, and happiness.

8. Cibella Borges had been a police officer in New York City for more than eighteen months when nude photographs of her appeared in a girlie magazine. (The photographs had been taken before she was appointed to the department.) She was subsequently dismissed from the department for "conduct prejudicial to the good order and effectiveness of the Police Department."[7]

9. A columnist on a college newspaper writes a column praising the American Nazi party and arguing that the security of the United States depends on the elimination of Jews, blacks, and Catholics from positions of importance and influence. Someone on the staff notifies the dean of student affairs that the column is scheduled for publication, and the dean forbids the editor to publish it.

10. A police officer is on duty in the station house when he overhears the victim of a robbery describing the robber to the desk sergeant. The officer realizes that the description fits his older brother perfectly. He pretends not to have heard the discussion.

11. Eight-year-old Tom receives a new and expensive toy from his parents for his birthday. They emphasize that they expect him to take special care of it. While playing with his friends, Tom notices that one boy keeps staring at the new toy. Realizing that the boy is poor and would be thrilled to have such a toy, Tom gives it to him to keep.

12. A young police officer is assigned to plainclothes duty in a local college. She attends classes, lives in a dormitory, and cultivates friendships with many students. Through those friendships she identifies the campus drug pushers, "sets them up," and arrests them.

13. A team of doctors has been assigned the difficult duty of deciding which of two patients will receive the next heart transplant when a heart is available. The patients are Anne, 12 years old, the only child of a laborer and his wife; and Mark, 48, an executive and the father of four children. They choose Anne.

14. An 18-year-old student, home from college during the semester break, stumbles on the fact that his father, whom he thought to be a business machines salesman, is actually a gunman for the mob. Moreover, he recently killed a member of a rival mob faction. The son considers going to the police and turning his father in, but he does not do so.

15. Raoul is a private detective. He specializes in cases in which husbands or wives suspect their mates of infidelity. In the performance of his service, he hides microphones in offices and homes (including bedrooms), breaks into homes and searches for incriminating evidence, and steams open private correspondence.

16. Two weeks ago Arthur was hospitalized for a series of tests. Yesterday the doctor called his wife in and explained that he has a fatal disease and has at most six months to live. The doctor adds that, in his judgment, Arthur would experience great difficulty coping with the truth. Today, sensing that something is troubling his wife, Arthur guesses and probes, "You're hiding something, aren't you, Martha? Is it about my tests? Am I going to die?" She has never lied to him and cannot bring herself to lie now. She tells him the truth.

17. Some time ago a man placed an ad in a newspaper seeking a young woman who would be willing to become pregnant for a $10,000 fee plus expenses and other benefits. The replies numbered in the thousands. He then explained to those who were interested that he represented a couple who could not have children. The plan was for the husband to impregnate the volunteer and then, nine months later, the couple would adopt the child. Among the reasons offered by the volunteers were the following: (a) a divorced woman wanted the money for a down payment on a house, (b) a married woman wanted the money to put her husband through school, (c) another married woman wanted to supplement the family income, (d) a single medical student wanted to finance the remainder of her education.[8] (Consider each volunteer's situation separately.)

18. A social caseworker learns that one of her clients is secretly playing in a band two nights a week and earning $20 a night. Since the client is physically disabled and receiving full welfare benefits for himself and his family, he is required by law to surrender any other income to the welfare department. He is breaking the law by keeping the money. The caseworker, knowing that the welfare benefits are based on an unrealistically low cost-of-living index, does not report the man.

19. Elvira is very much in love with her fiancé, Ethelred. Though they have been engaged for over a year (and sexually intimate for almost as long), Ethelred balks at setting a date for the marriage. Elvira is convinced that his obstacle is not disaffection, but fear, and once he can be moved to action, he will be relieved and happy. She therefore feigns pregnancy and plans to feign a miscarriage after they are married.

20. A man is elected to the presidency of a small country. Soon after his inauguration, he begins quietly to undermine the other branches of government and to assume more and more power himself. Within a few years his control is absolute. A large army and secret police force assure that his will is obeyed. Taxes rise, private businesses are taken over by the government, the standard of living of the average citizen plummets to a mere subsistence level. Protests are met with imprisonment and, in some cases, execution. A small band of men and women assassinate the tyrant and a half dozen of his lieutenants.

21. A high school basketball coach has a rule against smoking. Any team member who is caught violating the rule is supposed to be dropped from the team for the remainder of the season. Several days before the big game of the season, the game that will determine the league championship, the coach catches a star player violating the rule. He decides not to suspend him.

22. On October 13, 1972, a plane crashed high in the Andes mountains, killing almost two-thirds of its forty-five passengers and crew and leaving the others exposed to below-zero temperatures and the threat of starvation. More than three months passed before they were found. After their rescue it was revealed that the survivors had resorted to eating the flesh of their dead companions as a means of survival.[9]

23. Sharon and her friend Bill are both lab technicians in a blood bank. Sharon knows that Bill is going through a pretty tough divorce and that Bill's work hasn't been up to par. Sharon accidentally learns that Bill has mixed up several patients' blood samples. If Sharon corrects the errors, the director of the blood bank will find out and Bill will be fired. If she doesn't correct them, several doctors will receive incorrect information about their patients' physical condition. Sharon decides to report the errors.

24. Tina and Frank apply for the same job. Tina is the more qualified applicant, but Frank is the personnel officer's friend and next-door neighbor. The personnel officer knows that Frank's family needs the income badly. She screens out Tina and sends only Frank to interview with the boss.

CHAPTER TEN

CONSIDERING CONSEQUENCES

*How do we deal with cases in which the conse-
quences are not neatly separable into good and
bad, but are mixed?*

The relationship between actions and consequences is a cause-and-effect relationship, but not the kind we associate with the motion of physical objects, such as a row of dominoes tumbling down in predictable response to the falling of the first one. In human affairs the responses are never completely predictable. If Lucy curses Pauline, Pauline might well respond in kind; but then again, she might bless Lucy instead. If Clyde strikes Hector, chances are Hector will strike back, but it is possible that he will turn the other cheek. Similarly, some people who grow up in crime-ridden, drug-infested neighborhoods become criminals or drug users, but others remain honest and drug-free.* And though children who have been neglected or abused by their parents often harbor anger and resentment throughout their lives, in some cases animosity gives way to forgiveness and love.

The main difference between the laws of cause and effect in the physical universe and cause and effect in human affairs is that humans have the capacity to choose how they respond to events. To be sure, natural endowment and social conditioning exert a powerful influence and make some patterns of response more likely than others. (In Chapter 4 we

*For a fascinating and highly readable study that debunks media stereotypes of inner-city neighborhoods, see Mitchell Dunier's award-winning *Slim's Table: Race, Respectability, and Masculinity* (Chicago: University of Chicago Press, 1992).

discussed how these forces influence the development of conscience.) But in the vast majority of cases, these forces only *diminish,* rather than eradicate, one's freedom to choose.

Let's be clear that free will doesn't suspend the laws of nature. If a woman jumps out a fiftieth-floor window, she is not likely to get up and walk away, no matter how robust her will to survive. If a man sprinkles his mashed potatoes with cyanide, we can safely bet that he won't report for work tomorrow no matter how strong his intention to finish the project on his desk. (Chances are, he won't even make it through dessert!) Free will applies only in situations where response is possible; in those situations it enables people to resist outside influences, defy psychological and sociological axioms, and behave unpredictably.

□ DEALING WITH PROBABILITY

The fact that people can and do behave unpredictably makes consideration of consequences more difficult than it might otherwise be. Often as not, we are unable to arrive at certainty but must be content with probability. A case introduced earlier (Chapter 1, inquiry 7) will illustrate. That case recounted the poignant situation of a young girl who was raised by foster parents from infancy and then, at age 9, returned by court order to the former drug addicts who had neglected her. The effects that must be considered in this situation include those on the real parents, the foster parents, and the girl herself. The effects on the real parents, of course, are beneficial. They gain a purpose for living and for remaining off drugs. They can overcome the terrible sense of loss and of failure that must have plagued them since their child was taken from them. Unfortunately, the foster parents experience almost the opposite effect: a feeling of helplessness, a profound sense of loss, and perhaps a bitterness about the seeming unfairness of the court decision.

The obvious effect on the little girl is sadness and confusion at being separated from the only real parents she has ever known and at being given, like some inanimate object, to two strangers. But a deeper, delayed effect is also possible. Such an experience could leave an emotional scar on her. Will she be made bitter and cynical about human relationships? Will she be driven inward, avoiding the sharing of love and affection with others because of the subconscious fear that they, too, may be taken from her? Will she be filled with resentment toward her real parents and turn against them and all they try to do for her?

Each of these possibilities is very real. Although there is always the chance that none of them may happen, and instead her suffering may enrich her life and her trauma may lead her to become deeply sensitive to the sufferings of others, such a happy ending seems rather unlikely. The effect of lasting emotional damage is more probable and is thus the best measure of the morality of the court's action.

□ MAKING THE ANALYSIS THOROUGH

For moral judgment to be reliable, all significant consequences must be identified—the indirect as well as the direct, the subtle as well as the obvious, the unintended as well as the intended, the delayed as well as the immediate, the emotional and intellectual as well as the physical. The temptation to judge quickly and/or self-servingly poses a serious obstacle to thorough analysis.

Chapter 4, inquiry 7f, for example, presented the case of Fred, the son of a widow with seven children, who pays his way to college by stealing and selling automobile tires, radios, and stereo tape decks. He has decided that his behavior is justified because it helps him without hurting others: the owners are a bit inconvenienced, he reasons, but the insurance companies replace the stolen property.

Fred's examination of the consequences of his action is shallow. He has recognized only one dimension of one effect. There are other dimensions of that effect, and other effects, to consider. There is the effect on the insurance companies and their stockholders—making them pay for the stolen items. There is the effect on all the people who take out insurance policies with that company—making them pay higher premiums. There is the effect on every citizen's attitudes—contributing to fear and anger and suspicion. Not least there are the effects on Fred himself—reinforcing the habit of solving problems the easy way, blurring his sense of right and wrong, stilling his conscience with excuses and rationalizations.

To ensure that you account for all significant consequences, develop the habit of using your imagination: Visualize the action taking place at a particular time and place, and ask probing questions. In this case, some of the appropriate questions would have been, Who reimburses the victims of Fred's crimes? Where does the money come from? What is the public reaction to such crimes?

□ WHEN HARM IS UNAVOIDABLE

In some situations a beneficial effect and a harmful effect are inseparably joined; that is, either choice will produce an undesired effect as well as a desired one. Consider this case. Sophie has been kidnapped. For three days she has been held captive in a shack in the mountains, hoping that the ransom will be paid and she will be released. But now her captor is planning to kill her. "I'm really sorry, but I can't take the chance that you'll identify me," he says, as he unties her legs and orders her to walk out of the cabin. Just then, hearing a noise outside, he turns to look out the window. Sophie, her hands still tied, grabs the bread knife lying on the counter and stabs him in the back again and again until he falls dead at her feet.

Sophie's act was intentional murder. Yet it was morally justifiable because of what is called *the principle of the double effect*. This principle states that an act that produces a serious harmful effect is nevertheless morally acceptable if the harmful effect is not desired for itself, but is inseparable from the good effect that is sought. In Sophie's case she did not stab the kidnapper because she wanted to kill him, but because she wanted to protect herself from being killed. Thus she was really choosing the good effect and tolerating the harmful effect.*

This principle is neither new nor radical. In fact, it is a rather old and conservative ethical approach. It has, for instance, traditionally been applied by Roman Catholic ethicists in cases of fallopian pregnancy. In such abnormal pregnancies, the fetus fails to move down the fallopian tube and lodge in the uterus. Instead, it lodges in the fallopian tube itself. If it cannot be dislodged and made to continue on its course to the uterus, it will develop in the tube and cause the woman to hemorrhage and die. Despite the well-known Catholic opposition to induced abortion, in such cases Catholic ethicists approve surgical removal of the nonviable fetus. They reason that the unintended harmful effect of destroying the fetus is inseparable from the intended good effect of preserving the mother's life.

☐ THE GREATER GOOD

In situations involving mixed consequences, as in situations involving conflicting ideals, the morally preferable action is the one that will produce *the greater good* or, in cases where no good can be achieved, *the lesser harm*. Two examples from World War II will illustrate this principle. In the

---

*This principle does not apply in situations where the harm that is done is out of proportion to the good that is achieved. It could not, for example, be used to justify killing a roommate to stop her from using your clothes without permission.

North African theater of operations many hospitalized soldiers awaited the arrival of the first large shipment of the new wonder drug penicillin. When it arrived, high military medical officials had to decide which of two groups of patients to use it on, those with infected battle wounds or those with sulfa-resistant gonorrhea. Those with gonorrhea got the penicillin. The decision may at first seem absurdly wrong. But consider the reasoning that led to it. Large numbers of gonorrhea victims were crowding hospitals and posing the threat of infection to others. Within a week these men could be returned to the battle lines where, because there was a shortage of manpower and because victory was not yet assured, they were badly needed.[1]

The dilemma the medical officials faced was certainly unfortunate, and the choice they made unquestionably caused harm. But it was undoubtedly the right choice in that situation because the alternative choice would have caused more harm. Giving the penicillin to the gonorrhea victims served the greater good.

The second example is the U.S. decision to drop atomic bombs on Hiroshima and Nagasaki. At that time the war was still raging in the Pacific theater and, though the Japanese offensive had been rolled back, surrender was not expected. One option considered by the United States was an invasion of mainland Japan; this idea was rejected because the invasion would likely have been followed by a protracted military campaign and the combined cost in Japanese and American lives that would have resulted was conservatively estimated at several hundred thousand. The atomic bomb option was chosen because it would shorten the war by many months and would result in less death and destruction. Given just this information, we might conclude that the decision to use the atomic bomb represented, at the very least, the lesser evil. But the consequences were considerably more complex.

Whereas most of the individuals who would have been killed in an invasion would have been combatants, the overwhelming majority of the victims of the bombing were noncombatants. Nor was this an accidental matter—Hiroshima and Nagasaki were selected precisely because they were not military targets and their destruction would therefore have a greater demoralizing effect on the Japanese people. (Incidentally, the choice of civilian population centers violated a centuries-old prohibition.) The combined total killed in the two cities was over 200,000; tens of thousands of others suffered harmful exposure to radiation that caused them searing pain and disfigurement and could affect their children and grandchildren.

Other options existed that would have diminished the harmful effects. A single bomb could have been dropped on an uninhabited island as a demonstration of the destructive force of the bomb; the United States could have demanded that the Japanese surrender or face similar devastation. (Since the number of bombs was limited and an extended period of time was necessary to create more, this plan was rejected.) Or the first bomb could have been dropped on an exclusively military target and more time allowed for surrender terms to be met, in the hope that a second bombing would not be necessary. That this option was available suggests that the decision to bomb Hiroshima and Nagasaki did not represent the lesser evil.

The question of the greater good/lesser evil arises, of course, not just in dramatic situations but in many everyday situations like the following one:

For the first time in his twenty years as a high school football coach, Barney Bloom is looking forward with confidence to a winning season. His running back, Phil Blaster, is an athletic phenomenon. He has speed, power, cunning. Then, with practice scheduled to begin in three days, Bloom's bubble bursts. In examining Phil, the team doctor has detected a serious knee condition. His report, backed by a specialist who has studied the X rays, is that there will be great risk in Phil's playing this season. If the knee sustains a hard jolt from the right angle, Phil may never be able to play football again. Both doctors advise Phil to undergo surgery at once, but they leave the decision to him and his parents. Coach Bloom, determined to have Phil in his lineup, attempts to persuade Phil to wait until the football season is over to have the operation. Is Coach Bloom behaving morally? Let's examine the consequences and decide.

If Phil plays football without further injury to his knee, the team will undoubtedly have a winning season, the coach and all the players will achieve satisfaction, and the student body will experience the feeling of pride that accompanies having a winning team. Phil himself may benefit greatly by arousing the interest of college coaches and paving the way for an athletic scholarship to college. On the other hand, if Phil plays and gets injured, he may have no chance at a college career. Thus the possible good effects to the coach, the team, the school, and even to Phil himself must be weighed against the possible harmful effect to Phil.

The balance certainly seems to tip in favor of the coach's attempting to persuade Phil to postpone the operation. A greater number of people will benefit if Phil plays. But does benefiting the greater number constitute serving the greater good in this case? Further reflection raises serious questions about whether it does. Both the team doctor and a specialist decided that there was great risk in Phil's playing. One hard jolt from the right angle might finish Phil's career. If the sport were tennis or baseball, such a jolt might be considered unlikely to occur. But in football it is more than likely.

The fact that further injury to Phil's knee is probable if he decides to play, the fact that such an injury would end a promising career, and the fact that both doctors have recommended immediate surgery suggest that Coach Bloom's attempt to persuade Phil to play does not serve the greater good and is therefore immoral.

□ A CAUTION

As difficult as it is to deal with the observable good and evil consequences of already completed actions, it is even more difficult to consider the consequences of contemplated or hypothetical actions. Therefore, whenever we deal with what is contemplated or hypothetical, it is wise to keep the following caution in mind:

However clear and logical our determination of consequences may be, it is a prediction of future events and not a certainty. The particular set of responses that occurs and the changes in the thoughts, attitudes, and behavior of everyone affected by the action are intricate and sometimes, in some ways, unpredictable. Thus we are dealing with probabilities at best. For this reason, we must be thorough in accounting for all possible consequences and willing to modify our earlier judgments as actual consequences become available for our examination.

□ DEALING WITH DILEMMAS

Many of the cases we have considered in this and previous chapters have been frustrating to deal with. No solution seemed completely satisfying. No matter which we chose, we were left with the feeling that somehow there ought to be a better solution, even though we couldn't imagine what it might be. There is a formal name for this disquieting situation. It is called a *moral dilemma* and is defined as any predicament that arises from the impossibility of honoring all the moral values that deserve honoring. A moral dilemma exists whenever the conflicting obligations, ideals, and consequences are so very nearly equal in their importance that we feel we cannot choose among them, even though we must.

Moral dilemmas do not exist only in textbooks. They confront us in everyday life. They are a reality we must be prepared to deal with. We can never be completely comfortable in dealing with such dilemmas, but it is a consolation and source of confidence to remind ourselves from time to time that the frustration we experience with them is not a sign of incapacity on our part, but rather a reflection of the complex nature of moral discourse.

▦ INQUIRIES

1. What consequences does divorce produce? Make your list as complete as possible. Then consider relevant obligations and ideals and decide whether divorce is ever morally justifiable. (If you decide that it is in certain circumstances but not in others, specify each set of circumstances and explain your reasoning.)

2. Several years ago a married couple, faced with the tragic fact that the husband had terminal cancer, made an important decision: His sperm would be frozen so that the wife could conceive their child after his death. Three months after his death she was impregnated with his sperm and subsequently gave birth to a little girl. The Social Security Administration ruled that the child was not entitled to receive benefits as his heir. At first thought, you might be inclined to judge this ruling morally insupportable because the ideal of fairness requires that this child be treated as any other heir. Resist that judgment until you have used your imagination to identify the significant consequences that would likely follow (a) denying the child the status of heir and (b) granting the child the status of heir. Compare those consequences and make your decision.

3. What are the probable consequences of each of the following actions? (Try to identify all the consequences: direct and indirect; immediate and delayed; physical and emotional. If you are uncertain what the consequences are, consult knowledgeable people.) In each case, decide whether the favorable ones outweigh the unfavorable.

a. A rap music group creates song lyrics that recommend assaulting women.

b. A comedian specializes in material that ridicules blacks, Hispanics, and homosexuals.

c. A parents' group announces it will boycott companies that sponsor television programming that offends their moral values.

d. A movie studio produces X-rated films.

e. A school district uses a merit pay system; in other words, it awards salary increases on the quality of teaching performance, as measured by student and administrative evaluation.

f. Beer and liquor companies sponsor athletic contests. For example, Anheuser-Busch sponsors women's beach volleyball, Miller Brewing Company sponsors men's, and Southern Comfort sponsors a national "Finger Flick" tournament.

4. In each of the following cases, identify the consequences of the action taken and decide whether the action represented the greater good.

a. A college instructor is pursuing her doctorate in night school. To gain extra time for her own studies, she gives her students the same lectures, the same assignments, the same examinations semester after semester, without the slightest effort to improve them.

b. A physician on the staff of an urban medical center is approached by a lawyer from a remote part of the state and asked to testify on behalf of his client, a rural doctor charged with criminal negligence in the care of a patient. The lawyer admits that his client is guilty of the charge. He goes on to explain that although the doctor is old and not well versed in the latest medical knowledge, she is nevertheless competent; the negligence she is charged with resulted from the strain of being the only doctor in a large mountain area with a number of tiny towns and a total population of two thousand people. The lawyer pleads with the medical center physician to testify that the negligent act was proper treatment. The physician does so.

c. John and Martha, both married and the parents of several children, are having an adulterous affair. One night when they are meeting secretly, they witness a murder. They agree that they cannot report it without exposing their affair. The next day the body is found and within a week a suspect is apprehended and charged with first-degree murder. When John and Martha see his picture in the newspaper, they realize that he is not the murderer. They meet again, discuss their dilemma, and decide that despite the new, dreadful development, they will not step forward as witnesses.

d. An English teacher in a two-year technical college has several students in his composition course whose ignorance of the English language has proved invincible. He has given them extra work and extra counseling from the first week of the semester. They have been diligent in their efforts to improve. Though they are in a construction technology program and will undoubtedly be employed in jobs that require little writing skill, the composition course is required for graduation. In the instructor's judgment, the students would not be able to pass the course legitimately if they took it three times, so he raises their F grades to D's.

e.   Regina is chairperson of her city's United Fund campaign. In her annual meeting with her staff of canvassers, she gives this advice: "Hit the business places first. Don't approach anyone who is walking alone in a hall or working alone in a closed office. Look for two or more people standing together or working side by side. Try to make them compete with each other in giving. Capitalize on their desire to show off and outdo the next person."

f.   A senator has a bill before the Senate that promises to correct tax inequities that affect thousands of workers. However, the bill is being held up in committee. The committee chairperson is responsible. The senator, however, has learned of a secret scandal in the chairperson's personal life. He visits the chairperson and tells him that unless the bill is released from committee, he will divulge the scandal to the press.

g.   By day Sylvester is a high-ranking executive in a leading lingerie company. By night he is a modern Robin Hood. He scales walls and creeps over rooftops to enter the homes of the wealthy and steal cash and valuables. Everything he takes he gives to the poor.

h.   Jake runs a delicatessen in a high-crime section of a large city. After being robbed at gunpoint eight times in the past two years, Jake obtained a pistol permit and bought a pistol. Yesterday a man entered the store brandishing a knife and demanded all the money in the cash register. Jake moved to the cash register as if planning to open it. Then he quickly grabbed the gun hanging under it and, without warning, shot the man six times in the chest.

i.   After a young college instructor submits her final grades, she receives a music CD from two students with whom she has become quite friendly outside of class. The note accompanying the gift explains that it is a token of their gratitude for the instructor's presenting such an interesting and meaningful course. She keeps the compact disc.

j.   Todd and Edna have been married for three years. They have had serious personal problems: Edna is a heavy drinker, and Todd cannot keep a job. Also, they have bickered and fought constantly since their marriage. Deciding that the way to overcome their problems is to have a child, they stop practicing birth control, and Edna becomes pregnant.

k.   A member of the House of Representatives is encouraged by a big-business lobbyist to vote for a bill that is against the interests of her constituents. The lobbyist implies that if the representative supports the bill, big business will support her campaign for reelection. The representative knows that she faces a tough campaign against an unprincipled opponent. Without the support or at least the neutrality of big business, she has virtually no chance of reelection. She decides to support the bill.

l.   A company has a policy of strongly encouraging all workers over the age of 55 to retire in order to allow younger workers to be hired and advanced within the company. The company pension is modest, but a retiree can survive on it.

m.   A fiberglass firm is the only major employer in a small community. Officials are aware that the firm's safety practices are lax and that assembly workers suffer a variety of respiratory problems due to fumes and exposure to toxic materials. However, no action is ever taken against the company.

n.   A major aircraft manufacturer is dependent on government and private contracts. In good times it offers bonuses and recruits technical employees throughout the United States. In lean times the company engages in mass layoffs. Employees and technicians may be laid off within a year of moving their families across the country for a job.

o.   A college receives reduced operating funds. It closes its on-campus day-care center to save money for funding academic and technical instruction. The center previously served many low-income families.

5. In the inquiries on conscience, we considered the case of a candidate for the local school board, who was running against another candidate. She had heard the rumor that her opponent gave "wild parties." As she proceeded with her campaign, she visited the homes of many voters. She made it a point to tell everyone what she had heard about her opponent, always adding, "Of course, it's only a rumor that no one has yet proven to be true." Reexamine this case, focusing on the effects of her action.

6. In Chapter 3, inquiry 4, we considered the case of the Little League baseball coach who discovered a new boy in the neighborhood who was an excellent pitcher, though he was over the age limit for Little League participation. Because the family was not known in the area, the coach was sure he could use the boy without being discovered and ensure a winning season for his team. Reexamine this case, focusing on the effects of the action the coach planned.

CHAPTER ELEVEN

DETERMINING MORAL RESPONSIBILITY

How do we determine whether a person is responsible for her or his immoral actions? Are there degrees of responsibility?

The previous ten chapters focused on moral actions. This chapter examines a separate matter that is also of interest to ethicists, the issue of people's culpability (blameworthiness) for their actions. We noted in Chapter 1 that ethicists, unlike law enforcers, are not required to answer the question of a person's guilt or innocence in every moral issue they deal with. No ethics courts exist to render formal judgments of persons. Nevertheless, as we also noted, ethicists' insights in such matters provide guidance even for jurists.

The distinction between the act and the person who performs it is often misunderstood. When someone commits a moral offense, particularly a grievous one like assault or murder, justice would seem to demand that the person be held fully accountable. The moral perspective of many people is expressed in the legal maxim "the punishment should fit the crime." The notion that moral or legal responsibility can be diminished because of the circumstances in which the offense was committed may seem to compromise justice and condone immorality and lawlessness. This interpretation is understandable but mistaken. As we will see, fairness and honesty demand that circumstances be considered in determining culpability and that this determination has *no bearing on the judgment of the act*. An immoral act remains so even if the person who performs it is completely absolved of moral blame.

□ WHEN CULPABILITY IS DIMINISHED

Moral situations, as we have seen, involve choice. Obviously, when a person knows the quality of the action and makes a choice free from any compulsion,* he or she is morally responsible for the action. These favorable circumstances, however, are not always present. When they are not, the person is not morally responsible. Moral *guilt* can exist only where there is prior knowledge of the wrongness of the action.

The young child who sees one person stab another on television and then, in imitation, picks up a kitchen knife and stabs his sister, is not morally responsible at all. Neither is the severely retarded teenager who, while shopping with her mother, steals an expensive watch. They lack both an understanding of the nature of their behavior and the mental development to make an informed choice.

Similarly, we cannot assign blame to the prisoner of war who is tortured into revealing military secrets he swore to keep or to a crime witness who does not step forward because the criminal has threatened to harm her family if she does. In both these cases, the people are acting under duress, compelled to behave as they do by forces outside themselves. In other words, they have little or no freedom of choice.

Traditionally, it has been thought that psychopaths suffer from similarly diminished capacity for free choice, though the forces that influence them are internal rather than external. If this is so, then some of history's most infamous characters may not have been entirely responsible for their actions. Gilles de Rais, for example, the fifteenth-century marshal of France and patron of the arts who ritually murdered as many as 200 kidnapped children, may have been acting compulsively. Even Adolf Hitler, whose monstrous record of evil staggers the imagination—nearly 10 million human beings wantonly exterminated and the entire world plunged into strife, suffering, and destruction—may not have been fully responsible for his deeds. (There is evidence to suggest that he was emotionally disturbed.) Ironically, the moral responsibility of sane people who acted in his behalf was greater, even though the scale of their crimes was considerably smaller than his.

Not all evidence supports the traditional notion, however. Some authorities believe that psychopaths enjoy more freedom to choose than has been thought. One such individual is Stanton E. Samenow, a clinical psychologist specializing in criminal behavior. (Samenow and his col-

---

*As explained earlier, the idea of *complete* freedom is an illusion. Our genes and our conditioning limit our freedom to some extent. The question considered here is whether that normal degree of freedom is *further limited* in the particular situation.

league, Samuel Yochelson, authored the highly regarded three-volume study, *The Criminal Personality*.) Samenow believes the extensive literature on psychopathology has drawn an inaccurate picture of the psychopath. He writes:

> To say that a psychopath or criminal is unable to profit from experience is misleading because there is no such *incapacity*. He does learn from the past, but he learns what interests him, not what society wants him to learn. To call him impulsive is to assert that he lacks self-control, whereas he actually has a rational, calculating mind that is very much in control. Conscience is present and the criminal has moral values, but he shuts off his conscience long enough to do what he wants.[1]

John Douglas, author of an investigative study of serial killers, including David Berkowitz, Ted Bundy, and others, has reached a similar conclusion. He discovered that most of the individuals he studied were abused as children, later read pornographic material, and fantasized about how they would abuse others, findings that could be interpreted as signs of compulsion. Yet he also found that most were bright—Ted Bundy's IQ was over 125, and Edmund Kemper's was 145—and most could tell right from wrong. They committed their crimes not because of irresistible impulse but because they simply didn't give a damn about others and enjoyed inflicting pain.[2]

In situations where the evidence is insufficient to determine whether a particular person acted freely, prudence precludes judgment. Nevertheless, we can assert with conviction that *if* a person's freedom to act is diminished, then his or her culpability is diminished to that extent.

☐ ETHICS AND LAW

The conflicting evidence concerning the psychopath's freedom of choice has complicated the legal approach to insanity cases. In the 1980s public concern over the wisdom of the insanity plea in American law reached a peak with the decision that John Hinckley, who had shot the president of the United States and three other men, was "not guilty by reason of insanity." The cries for legal reform generated by such cases may result in change. (One possibility is the replacement of the present "not guilty by reason of insanity" plea with "guilty, but insane," which would prevent premature release from psychiatric detention.)

The legal tradition of distinguishing the compulsive criminal from the noncompulsive is not likely to change, however. The distinction is too deeply rooted in the moral tradition that it is unjust to hold a person responsible for actions over which he or she had little or no control.

☐ MORE TYPICAL CASES

Psychopathic behavior is not typical, of course. It may involve a total or nearly total lack of responsibility. In most moral situations the person acting has some knowledge of the quality of the act and at least some freedom of choice. The decision as to moral responsibility in such cases depends on the *degree* of that understanding and the *degree* of freedom of choice.

Consider this case. A neurotically insecure woman constantly seeks reassurance that she is attractive and desirable. As a result, she is very vulnerable to selfish, insensitive men. When, as happens frequently, a man uses her for his sexual pleasure and then casts her aside, the rejection makes her all the more insecure, all the more anxious to prove her attractiveness, and all the more vulnerable to other men.

Two of the men who have used her in this manner are a bartender at one of her haunts and her psychiatrist. The bartender didn't understand her problem. He saw her merely as a pretty and available woman. So he fed her a few drinks and a few smiling lies, enjoyed himself, and assumed that she did likewise. The psychiatrist, on the other hand, knew her condition very well. He also knew exactly what harm such experiences had on her emotionally. Yet, like the bartender, he calculated and carried out his sexual conquest. Assuming that neither man acted compulsively, which was more blameworthy? The psychiatrist was. Even though he used the woman no differently from the bartender, he understood the effects of his action more fully. He knew the harm he was causing. Moreover, he enjoyed a special relationship of trust with the woman and therefore was required to give special concern to her interests.

The same kind of distinctions can be made with freedom of choice. On the same day in the same area of the same war, three soldiers may perform an identical act, each of them killing an unarmed, unthreatening civilian. Yet differing circumstances may absolve one, partly absolve the other, and damn the third. The first, for example, may have been ordered directly by an officer to shoot the civilian or be shot himself; the second may have received the order indirectly and, not being observed, may have had a reasonable chance to disobey without threat to his own life; the third may have killed for pleasure. Our assignment of moral responsibility would be in proportion to the degree of freedom of each man's choice.

□ HEROISM NOT REQUIRED

In considering the question of moral blame, we should keep in mind that we can be good men and women without being heroes. Naturally, it is desirable to aim for the highest and noblest actions. But there is no moral requirement to do so. The only requirement implied in the concept of morality is to do good and avoid doing evil.

A case in point occurred during World War II. Soon after the Nazis occupied Austria, they drafted Austrian men into their armed services. One citizen they called was Franz Jägerstatter, a simple, uneducated man in his mid-30s with a wife and young children. Because he believed that Hitler's cause "offended God," he was convinced that it would be morally wrong for him to serve it, so he refused to be drafted. As a result, he was imprisoned. For months his friends, his parish priest, and even his bishop urged him to think of his family and reconsider his decision. They explained that in such a situation he was being forced to serve and not doing so voluntarily, so he would not be guilty of any wrongdoing. Despite their pleading, Jägerstatter remained steadfast in his conviction. Finally, he was executed.

Did he do wrong? Of course not. His loyalty to his convictions was admirable. He was a hero. But his friends' advice was not wrong either. They and the many who yielded to the Nazi pressure and answered the draft call were weaker than Jägerstatter. They lacked his courage. Yet they were not blameworthy because they did not choose freely.

Conscience also complicates the determination of guilt and innocence. We observed earlier that people must follow their conscience and therefore cannot be condemned for doing what it bids them. Yet conscience is an imperfect guide, capable of directing one to wrong as well as right behavior. It would appear, then, that it is not fair to blame a person for doing any wrong act that his or her conscience supports. Most ethicists would accept this conclusion, provided two conditions were met: (a) the person did not neglect the job of developing his or her conscience in a responsible way; (b) the person did nothing to desensitize his or her conscience.

▦ INQUIRIES

1. Is it morally wrong to read literature or listen to speeches sponsored by groups that promote hatred of racial, ethnic, or religious groups? Are there any special circumstances in which you would modify your view? Explain.

2. A husband and wife are walking across a railroad track. She stumbles and her foot gets caught in the switching mechanism. He tries to free her. Then a train comes roaring around the corner. Realizing he cannot free her before the train reaches them, the man leaps to safety. She is struck and killed instantly. Has the man behaved immorally? Why or why not?

3. In 1913 Leo M. Frank was found guilty of the murder of a 13-year-old girl in the pencil factory in which they both worked. He was sentenced to death. When his sentence was commuted to life imprisonment in 1915, an enraged mob hanged him. Sixty-seven years later, a witness to the crime came forward and testified that, as a 14-year-old boy, he had seen another man carrying the girl's body. He explained that he had not spoken out because the real murderer had threatened to kill him if he testified. Was that witness's silence morally justified?

4. A man is falsely accused of a crime and spends fourteen years in jail. Finally, his accuser is overcome with remorse and admits having lied. When the man is released, he sues the state for wrongful imprisonment and seeks monetary compensation. The courts rule that the state has no legal responsibility. But does it have *moral* responsibility? Why or why not?

5. In the 1950s and 1960s Navajo Indians and others worked in the uranium mines in New Mexico, Arizona, Utah, and Colorado. The Atomic Energy Commission (AEC) and the Public Health Service (PHS) allegedly knew that such work was hazardous. In the 1920s European studies had linked radioactivity to cancer and determined that ventilation of shafts could reduce the hazard. Also, U.S. research in the late 1940s revealed that cancer was also caused by inhaling radon gas. Yet neither agency pressured the mine owners to install safety devices and neither warned the workers. Moreover, the PHS monitored the health of a test group of miners; in the words of Stewart Udall, "The PHS used the miners as guinea pigs to study the effects of radiation." Today those workers develop lung cancer at a rate five times higher than that of other people.

6. When suit was brought against the U.S. government in the case detailed in inquiry 5, an appeals court ruled that the federal government was protected by sovereign immunity, meaning that the government can decide when and if it can be sued. Discuss the morality of sovereign immunity in this case.

7. For a group of people to stand by without intervening as a man beats a woman into unconsciousness and then kicks her brutally would surely be immoral. However, the moral responsibility of the crowd would depend on a number of considerations. Determine the degree of the crowd's responsibility in each of the following variations.

   a. The crowd is composed of very old men and women. The assailant is young, strong, and armed with an iron pipe.

   b. The crowd is composed of women 20 to 30 years of age. The assailant is unarmed.

   c. The crowd is a group of construction workers. The man is spindly, middle-aged, and unarmed.

8. A 7-year-old Virginia boy set fire to a building. As a result of the blaze, a 66-year-old woman died. The boy was charged with second-degree murder.[3] Could the boy be morally responsible for the crime of murder? If so, what circumstances might increase or reduce his responsibility?

9. A prominent Houston attorney, William Chanslor, Jr., was charged with solicitation of murder and conspiracy to commit murder after he contracted a professional assassin to murder his wife. At his trial Chanslor testified that his wife, having suffered a stroke that caused brain damage and paralyzed one side of her body, begged him repeatedly to help her commit suicide. He explained that he had initially tried to talk her out of the idea of suicide and changed his mind only after her constant begging for help.[4] Assuming the circumstances were as the attorney described them, to what extent do they lessen his moral responsibility?

10. Five New Jersey teenagers were drinking beer by the railroad tracks near their home when they heard a train approaching. They decided to throw a track switch and sent the train careening off the tracks, down a siding, and through the brick wall of a building. The crash killed the engineer, critically injured one passenger, and caused an estimated $5.5 million in property damage.[5] Discuss the teenagers' moral responsibility for their act in light of the circumstances in which it took place.

11. A college basketball team is heavily favored to win the forthcoming end-of-season tournament. Then the star player signs a professional contract and is no longer eligible to play with his team. Was his signing unethical? If so, what circumstances would lessen his responsibility?

12. The evidence that smoking is harmful to one's health continues to grow. Now smoking is linked not only to lung cancer, emphysema, and certain heart and artery conditions, but also to cancers of the bladder and pancreas. In addition, smoking by pregnant women has been linked to such fetal defects as low birth weight and poor general health. With these facts in mind, decide whether the following people commit any moral wrong and, if so, identify the circumstances in which each would be morally responsible.

   a.   The heavy cigarette smoker

   b.   The pregnant woman who smokes

   c.   The smoker who encourages a nonsmoker to start smoking

   d.   The farmer who grows tobacco

   e.   The cigarette distributor

   f.   The advertising person who creates ads to entice people into buying cigarettes

   g.   The well-known personality who lends her name to cigarette advertising

13. Is pushing heroin a moral offense? If so, is the moral responsibility of the heroin-using pusher any different from that of the nonusing pusher?

14. Louise is an investigator for the Internal Revenue Service. Her job consists of closely examining the tax returns of individuals selected at random by a computer. When she finds significant errors in the returns, she assigns penalties. Because the majority of the cases she handles involve middle-income families and because it is her strong conviction that the tax law discriminates against such people, Louise has begun to feel guilty for doing her job. Nevertheless, she refuses to quit. Is she doing wrong? If so, what is the degree of her moral responsibility?

15. A high school girl accuses a boy in her class of putting his hand up her dress. The boy is reported to the principal. The principal questions the boy and the girl. She must base her decision on these facts: There were no witnesses; the boy denies having touched the girl; the girl has made similar unsupported charges about other boys in the past. The principal is reasonably sure the boy is innocent. Nevertheless, she suspends him from school. Clearly, the principal has acted dishonestly. Speculate on the circumstances that might have been present to diminish her moral responsibility for her action.

16. A major pipeline is under construction. Federal inspectors discover that hundreds of improperly welded joints have been certified by state inspectors. To what degree is each of the following individuals responsible?

   a.   The owner of the construction company who paid the state inspector to certify the welding jobs

   b.   The state inspector who certified the welding

   c.   The supervisor of the job who carried out the boss's orders to have the work done by unqualified (and lower-paid) workers

   d.   The union steward who failed to make the situation known to authorities

17. All of the mechanics at a certain garage are expected to look for mechanical problems in addition to those presented by their customers. It is understood, but not discussed openly, that the mechanic will recommend unnecessary repairs if he can get away with it. To what degree are each of the following responsible for the continuation of this practice?

   a.   The garage owner who encourages these practices

   b.   The mechanic who does the work

   c.   The customer who, through mental laziness, continues to be ignorant of mechanical matters

III

THE TRADITION

CHAPTER TWELVE

A PERSPECTIVE ON HISTORY

When did the study of ethics begin? Who were the great thinkers in the history of ethics? What contributions did they make?

This chapter is as much a beginning as a conclusion. It opens the way for you to deepen your understanding of the subject of ethics, to become acquainted with some of the great ethical thinkers and thoughts of the past, even as you continue to apply your evaluative skills to the ethical problems of today. You will probably appreciate its contents more now than you would have if you had read it at the outset, for now you have struggled with numerous ethical issues yourself, felt the pull of conflicting values, wrestled with moral dilemmas to which no answer seems completely satisfactory. Now, too, you know the value of careful analysis and a systematic approach. This will enable you to appreciate the ideas advanced by the various ethicists as they attempted to construct an ethical system. Even when you do not share their philosophic perspective, you will understand their efforts and share their enthusiasm for the task.

Historians usually divide the history of ethics in Western thought into three large periods: the *classical,* the *medieval,* and the *modern.* Any division, naturally, is arbitrary. There are no real breaks in time; the flow of moment to moment is constant. Nevertheless, the divisions are convenient. They help us to grasp major developments more fully and see shifting focuses and changing perspectives more sharply.

☐ THE CLASSICAL PERIOD

The classical period of ethical thought extends from 500 B.C. to A.D. 500. At the beginning of this period a rapid change was taking place in Greek society. Once an agrarian monarchy, it was now becoming a commercial industrial democracy. New changes brought new challenges to old values and traditions. The ethics of the time reflected the central feature of the society, the city-state. Thus the moral focus was the duty of the individual as a citizen. Ethics was regarded as the spiritual counterpart of medicine, its function being to provide care of the soul as medicine provides care of the body.

With values in flux, a number of moral views arose to clash with the traditional view. The Sophists, a group of itinerant teachers, questioned to what extent morality was a matter of nature and to what extent a matter of custom or tradition. Their general view was that good and evil are matters of personal decision or social agreement. Some of the more liberal Sophists suggested that all morality was a matter of convenience only.

Socrates (469–399 B.C.) was the dominant figure of the classical period. Indeed, he is generally regarded as the father of Western philosophy. He left no writings, but many of his views were recorded in the writings of his pupil Plato. Like the Sophists, Socrates rejected the idea that tradition justifies conduct. But unlike them, he believed that morality is more than a matter of personal choice or convenience. It is possible, he believed, to develop a universal set of ethical principles to guide conduct, and the key to doing so is human reason, the careful examination of beliefs and actions and the logic that underlies them. His focus was on self-knowledge. "The unexamined life," he taught, "is not worth living."

Socrates is best known for his philosophic method. Rather than teach directly, he conversed with others, asking basic questions about important matters (for example, What is justice? What is virtue?) and then examining the answers people gave, exposing vagueness and inconsistency, clarifying problems, and pointing the way to further inquiry. He was also the first to probe the relationships between facts and values, an ethical issue that virtually all ethicists since his time have grappled with.

Plato (427–347 B.C.) built upon the teaching of Socrates. Plato's writings are in dialogue form, and Socrates is the main character in most of them. Plato's greatest work is *The Republic*. He shared Socrates' view that the life of reason is the happiest and best life. For both men sense perception and bodily pleasure were less desirable than intellectual pursuits, but the two men differed somewhat in their emphases. Socrates apparently believed in enjoying himself at all levels of experience in a balanced way. He believed that nothing should be done to excess, that moderation should be the rule in everything. Plato's view was more extreme. His denial of bodily pleasure and sense perception made him a model for later religious and idealistic ethicists.

Plato's central notion was that the real world is not the world that our senses perceive, but the world of ideas. The concrete reality that surrounds us, in Plato's view, is merely an imperfect reflection of the world of abstract ideas or "forms," which are timeless and unchanging. The most important reality in this world of ideas is the idea of the Good. Goodness for Plato was a central fact about the universe. Thus the main goal of his ethical system is to gain a vision of the Good.

Aristotle (384–322 B.C.) was a student of Plato and followed his and Socrates' philosophical tradition. Nevertheless, Aristotle's emphasis was quite different from Plato's. Aristotle authored as many as four hundred works on a variety of subjects from theoretical and practical science to politics, rhetoric, logic, and ethics. His *Nichomachean Ethics* is the first systematic treatment of ethics in Western civilization.

Aristotle disputed Plato's theory of forms. There is no world of separate, abstract forms corresponding to the concrete things we perceive, he reasoned. Form cannot exist apart from particular objects, or as he put it, "No form without matter, no matter without form." Accordingly, Aristotle rejected the notion that the Good exists independently of daily experience and human personality. In his view moral principles exist in the daily activities of human life and can be discovered by examining those activities. Happiness is to be attained by developing one's potential for a life of reason. The life of reason has two aims: the pursuit of truth through reflection and understanding and the pursuit of virtue through intelligent conduct. Virtue, for Aristotle, represented a midpoint between extremes of excess and defect. (Some actions, however, like murder or theft, he saw as bad in themselves and therefore having no midpoint.)

Not all thinkers of the classical period shared the philosophical tradition of Socrates, Plato, and Aristotle. The Cyrenaics, for example, and later the Epicureans emphasized human feelings and desires and taught that the measure of an action is the amount of *pleasure* it brings. (This view is known as *hedonism.*) Epicurus, however, made a sharp distinction between "natural" pleasures, such as peace of mind and the absence of hunger, and "unnatural" pleasures, such as greed and lust, approving only the former. In contrast to the Cyrenaics and Epicureans were the Cynics and then the Stoics. These groups stressed overcoming feelings and desires and serving the demands of *duty* as revealed by reason.

As we shall see, many of the differences in viewpoint that existed during the classical period, such as the difference over pleasure and duty, have continued to divide thinkers through the centuries.

☐ THE MEDIEVAL PERIOD

The second period in the history of ethics in the West is the medieval period, which extends from 500 to 1500. Its intellectual and social context was Christianity. As the belief system of Christianity (itself a product of Judaic thought) expanded across Europe, the idea of the citizen's relation to the state was replaced by the idea of the individual's obligation to God as set forth in the Bible and interpreted by the Church. Medieval ethics combined the classical emphasis on human reason with the idea of obedience to God's will.

Two great thinkers dominated medieval thought. The first was Saint Augustine (354–430). In his numerous works, notable among them *Confessions* and *The City of God,* Augustine made Plato's philosophy the basis of Christian ethics. Augustine's system was two-sided. On the one side, the life of reason leads to temporal well-being; on the other, faith leads to salvation and eternal happiness. (Since this life is only a preparation for the afterlife, Augustine taught, no real happiness is possible here.) The concept of Good for Augustine was similarly two-sided: the natural, earthly side and the supernatural, other-worldly side, with the supernatural dominating. Augustine viewed man as having fallen from God's grace through original sin but retaining free will and responsibility for his actions. Virtue is possible, he taught, but to have real value it must be prompted by faith.

The Platonic system of Augustine was so emphasized in the early Middle Ages that Aristotle was all but forgotten until the time of the second great medieval thinker, Saint Thomas Aquinas (1225–1274). Aquinas rediscovered Aristotle, Christianized his philosophy, and made it the basis of the philosophical outlook of the later Middle Ages. Aquinas's greatest works were *Summa Theologica* and *Summa Contra Gentes.*

Aquinas aimed at demonstrating the harmony between Aristotle and Christianity. He taught that ethics has two dimensions—the natural and the theological. Natural ethics, as detailed by Aristotle, consists of the development of reason and practice in living morally and leads to earthly happiness. Theological ethics consists of achieving the virtues of faith, hope, and charity through God's grace and leads to eternal life with God. Aquinas believed that the Natural Law—the divine law as written in the heart of man—can be discovered by reason and cultivated by conscience. By allowing people to turn to secular knowledge without guilt, Aquinas prepared the way for the emergence of a more scientific view of humanity and of ethics.

□ THE MODERN PERIOD

The third period in the history of ethics extends from 1500 to the present.* The sixteenth and seventeenth centuries were times of intellectual upheaval. The Protestant Reformation challenged the supremacy of the Roman Catholic church and introduced the idea of each person's interpreting the Bible for himself or herself. The impact of this idea was increased with the invention of the printing press and the shift from Latin to the vernacular. Finally, and perhaps most importantly, the work of scientists like Copernicus, Galileo, and Harvey turned the attention of philosophers from theological to scientific explanations.

Thomas Hobbes (1588–1679) was the first thinker to systematically approach ethics from a scientific viewpoint. Hobbes, whose major philosophical work was *Leviathan,* argued that the notion of mechanistic materialism that was central to the physics of the time applied to ethics as well. He attempted to demonstrate that in humanity's natural (primitive) condition the rule of self-preservation produces a morality based on *self-interest.* In that condition, Hobbes reasoned, the concepts of right and wrong do not exist; they only begin to exist when civil society is formed. The only way civil society can control the pursuit of individuals' self-interest and the conflict that such pursuit inevitably generates is to have everyone give allegiance to the sovereign. Hobbes believed in the Golden Rule, but he also believed that people could not be trusted to practice it. With too much at stake for each person to follow his or her conscience, Hobbes argued, the sovereign power—whether "monarch or assembly"—must ensure "the safety of the people."

There was strong reaction against Hobbes' ethical perspective. In refutation of that perspective a number of ethicists argued that human beings are not at the mercy of their drive for self-preservation. They have a moral faculty, a specific intellectual guide that enables them to tell right from wrong. Several different ways of describing that moral faculty were advanced. Some described it as *intuition,* others as a *moral sense* (a natural affection for virtue), and still others as *conscience.*

In the early eighteenth century David Hume (1711–1766) proposed an ethical theory that was in some ways reminiscent of John Locke's theory in the previous century. Locke (1632–1704) had argued that pleasure is the standard of moral judgment. Sensations of pleasure or pain, he reasoned,

*In some classifications the contemporary period (twentieth century) is accorded a separate category.

lead us to reflect and form views of justice and goodness and thus develop a system of moral judgment. Hume believed that the standard of moral judgment is two-sided. One part of it is objective—the consequences of the action in question. The other part, the dominant part, in Hume's view, is subjective—a feeling of pleasure. (Like most hedonistic philosophers, Hume did not approve of doing anything we wish. He believed that every human being possesses a tendency to be more pleased by benefiting others than by being selfish and self-indulgent.) In Hume's theory reason alone cannot answer moral questions. But a "moral sentiment" that chooses what is useful or pleasant can and does do so.

THE ETHICS OF DUTY (DEONTOLOGY)

The writings of Immanuel Kant (1724–1804) represent a significant milestone in modern ethics. Kant's main work was *Critique of Pure Reason*. However, it was in *The Fundamental Principles of the Metaphysics of Morals* that he set forth his views of the foundation of morality. Kant took issue with Hume's view about feeling and with the general position of all hedonists. He argued that moral judgments are not expressions of feeling, but *imperatives* (commands) and so can be dealt with by reasoning. To those skeptics who say that there is no certainty in moral judgment, Kant replied that it is incorrect to look for certainty in the *content of experience*. It can only be found in the *form of reason*. In other words, he believed that certainty does not come from observation, but is a product of mind.

Things that are usually called "good," such as intelligence, courage, and perseverance, are in Kant's terms only good if they are joined by the person's *goodwill* (that is, good character). It is goodwill that directs people to do what they *ought* to do rather than what they wish to do or what will benefit them. Although Kant acknowledged that happiness is desirable, he suggested that reason can never achieve happiness; it can only achieve a goodwill.

According to Kant, the basis of moral action is *duty*. People's goodwill is what makes them act for duty, and acting for duty gives their action moral value. The central thesis of Kant's ethical system is that there is a "categorical imperative" (command) binding on all people because it is affirmed by reason, and every rational person accepts his or her obligation to follow reason. Kant expressed this categorical imperative as follows, the first formulation being the principal one:

> Act as if the maxim of your action were to become by your will a universal Law of Nature [to be obeyed by everyone].

Always treat every human being, including yourself, as an end in himself and never merely as a means to an end.

THE ETHICS OF CONSEQUENCES (TELEOLOGY)

Another significant milestone in modern ethics is the work of John Stuart Mill (1806–1873). Unlike many of the ethicists we have discussed, Mill did not create a system of ethics himself. He clarified and defended a system created earlier by his father, James Mill, and by Jeremy Bentham. That system is called *utilitarianism,* and its central premise is that the rightness or wrongness of actions is determined by the goodness or badness of their consequences. John Stuart Mill's most famous work is his *System of Logic,* but it is his essay *Utilitarianism* that deals specifically with ethics.

Mill's utilitarianism is a hedonist ethics. (In other words, it makes pleasure or happiness the standard of moral judgment.) Specifically, utilitarianism states that "Utility, or the Greatest Happiness Principle" is the foundation of morals. Mill admitted that some pleasures are of a higher type than others, and he suggested that competent judges who have experienced both kinds of pleasure will be found to prefer the higher over the lower. He acknowledged too, that some people choose to follow the principle of utility because they seek the favor of friends and neighbors or they fear the wrath of God. However, such external motivations are secondary to the ultimate, internal motivation: *an inner feeling for humanity.* This feeling expresses what has been termed a *generalized benevolence,* an attitude that everyone's happiness is equal and one's own happiness should not be pursued at others' expense.

Though Mill himself believed that the inner feeling for humanity is acquired rather than inborn, he did not feel it important to demonstrate the point. Whether acquired or inborn, he explained, makes little difference. The main point for him was that it does exist, that it is a powerful sentiment, and that in its focus on the happiness of all people it constitutes the most solid ethical standard.

Since the time of Mill, numerous ethical theories have been advanced. One important focus of this time has been on the logic of discourse; that is, on the language used to express moral judgments and the logical implications of that language. Notable among more recent theories has been the "Good Reasons" approach taken by such contemporary philosophers as Stephen Toulmin, Kurt Baier, Kai Nielsen, and John Rawls. The central focus of that approach has revolved around this question: "When is a reason for a moral judgment a *good* reason?" These ethicists hold that the primary purpose of moral discourse is not to advance theories or to express individual perspectives, but to guide conduct.

□ GREAT ISSUES IN ETHICS

As even this brief survey makes clear, the history of ethics has been essentially the story of the search for a single satisfying standard against which to judge moral questions. That the search continues—even after almost 2500 years—may seem to imply that it has been a failure. That is surely not the case. Each contributor has advanced the cause of knowledge. If the task that the great ethicists set for themselves remains unfinished, it is only because of its magnitude. They were pursuing nothing less than the ultimate basis of moral judgment, the perfect explanation of morality.

Is such a perfect explanation possible? Perhaps, but many contemporary thinkers doubt it. Still, the paradoxical truth may be that progress in ethical understanding demands that we believe in the possibility and strive to realize it. We must, like Socrates, keep speculating, keep examining, keep questioning. In that spirit we will end this brief historical perspective with some of the most challenging questions that have occupied the attention of the great ethicists over the centuries.

Do human beings have a natural tendency to good, a natural tendency to evil, or some combination of tendencies? What are the implications of your answer for ethics?

What conditions must be present before we can say a person is truly happy? Which of these conditions are most important? What is the best expression of the relationship between ethics and happiness?

Is the preserving of one's dignity or the serving of a principle other than self-interest ever a higher good than personal happiness?

Is there any action that is good in itself, without reference to the consequences it brings about? Or does every good derive its value from its consequences?

Whose interests should be paramount in ethical judgment? One's own? Those of the people directly affected by the action? The interests of all humanity? Is the answer necessarily the same in all situations?

Are some acts morally obligatory regardless of the consequences for human benefit or harm?

How important is objectivity in moral judgment? To what extent can the process of moral judgment be objective?

Is there a single universal moral code that is binding upon all people at all times and in all places? If so, how are the differences in moral perspective to be accounted for? If not, how can people with different moral perspectives be expected to live in harmony and how is the notion of progress in ethics to be understood?

⊞ INQUIRY

Answer one or more of the preceding questions as your instructor directs. Be sure to consider all possible answers before choosing any one. Try to anticipate the objections that might be raised to your answer by those who disagree with you, and present an effective response to those objections.

IV

CONTEMPORARY
ETHICAL
CONTROVERSIES

□ EDUCATION

1. High schools around the country sometimes experience problems with censorship. In most cases school boards respond to community complaints that some books are immoral or un-American by banning those books from the school library. Is the censorship of books in schools ever morally justifiable?

2. Many colleges prohibit the drinking of alcoholic beverages on campus. Is such a prohibition morally justifiable?

3. Under what circumstances, if any, is it morally justifiable for grade school or high school teachers to hit students?

4. A complaint from a California state senator sparked a review of the Women's Studies Program at the California State University, Long Beach, campus. The senator charged that the instructor of a course entitled "Women and Their Bodies" showed the students in her class slides of her genitals and suggested that they imagine "doing things" with other women in the class.[1] Is either of these acts morally objectionable?

5. In education, as in business, mistakes are sometimes made in promoting a person. For example, a respected high school teacher with twenty years of service may be made principal of his school. After serving for a year in this new capacity, the man may have demonstrated clearly that he is incompetent in administrative affairs. But by that time his former teaching position will have been filled. Consider the various ethical considerations involved both in retaining him and in firing him, and decide what course of action and what conditions would be the most ethical solution for the school board.

6. Once in a while a case of a teacher who has taught for years with forged credentials comes to light. Once the deception is found out, of course, he or she is dismissed and may even be prosecuted. But consider the moral dilemma that must exist for the principal when he or she first learns of the lie. Suppose, for example, the principal learns that instead of having the master's degree the records indicate, the teacher dropped out of college after one year as an undergraduate. Further suppose that the teacher is by every measure one of the very best in the school. Should the principal expose the teacher or allow the deception to continue? Would your judgment change if the teacher were not outstanding but merely average?

7. In every academic subject there are areas of controversy, questions that different schools of thought answer differently. For example, in psychology there are Freudian, Jungian, and Adlerian perspectives; in literature there are several approaches to interpretation (such as the esthetic and the psychological). Is it ethically acceptable for an instructor to teach only the school of thought he or she personally accepts? Would your answer be different in the case of an introductory course than in the case of an advanced course?

8. In determining students' final grades, some college instructors use as one factor their personal, subjective judgment of students' effort and contribution to class discussion. The factor may vary in its weighting from 10 to 20 percent or even higher. Is this practice ethical? Under what conditions, if any?

9. More than a few college professors today believe that the very idea of a grading system is punitive and archaic. Some of them, however, are in the minority at their institutions and are therefore required to submit grades in their courses. One way to do so and still serve their consciences is to give everyone an A, regardless of the quality or quantity of the work he or she submits. Discuss the morality of this practice.

10. In most colleges the chairperson of an academic department is responsible to the academic dean. If the dean should, for example, criticize the chairperson's department for submitting too many low grades in a particular semester and demand that the department review its grading policy so that it can begin assigning "more reasonable" grades, the chairperson would have to decide how to deal with the matter. Each of the following is a possible approach. Evaluate the ethical character of each:

> **a.** The chairperson can call in each faculty member and review the member's grading policy with him or her in an attempt to determine whether the policy is too stringent.

> **b.** The chairperson can issue a memorandum to the department members explaining the dean's concern and desire that the department grades improve the next semester.

> **c.** The chairperson can issue a demand that each department member's grades conform in the future to the normal distribution curve.

11. Few colleges today are without their experimental courses or curriculums. In their most sophisticated form such courses or curriculums are run side by side with traditional ones so that their effectiveness can be compared. At the outset of such experiments, of course, it is impossible to be certain that the experiment will be even minimally effective. Are such experiments ethically permissible? If so, under what conditions?

12. A teacher is usually assigned to teach courses with specific content. He or she is expected to select or create lessons that will impart the knowledge and develop the skills that are associated with that content. To do other than that—for example, to teach economics instead of literature in a literature course—would clearly be to break his or her moral obligation to the students who enrolled for the advertised course. Yet in subtler cases the answer is not so clear. Would it violate that obligation if a chemistry professor presented a filmstrip on chemical weapons as part of an anti-war lecture? Would it violate that obligation if a math instructor spent one class period talking about the importance of population control? Why or why not?

13. Term paper ghostwriting is surely not a new idea. But doing it on the scale of big business, with advertisements in college newspapers, branch offices, and a stable of writers, is. It is possible today to buy a term paper on virtually any subject, complete with footnotes and bibliography. Some companies even offer tailor-made papers. Is such a business ethical?

14. Some time ago a young man filed a one-million-dollar lawsuit against the high school that graduated him, charging the school with legal responsibility for his inability to read and write adequately.[2] It seems unlikely that the courts would find the school legally responsible for his ignorance. But is it possible that the school is morally responsible? Under what conditions might it be?

15. Compulsory education, the required attendance of young people between certain ages (for example, between 5 and 16 in many states), has become a tradition in the United States. The idea that requiring young people to attend school is an infringement of their rights as citizens, a kind of slavery, is unthinkable to many Americans. Yet there are men and women, some of them respected educators, who are openly expressing that idea. They argue that children themselves, or at least their parents in their behalf, should decide whether they will attend school and, assuming they decide in the affirmative, where, what, and for how long the children will study. Consider the ethical side of the question. Are compulsory education laws morally wrong?

16. The age difference between teachers and students is sometimes relatively slight. A high school teacher could be 21 and a high school senior 17. A college instructor could be 25 and a college senior 22. Would it be unethical in any way for such teachers to date their students? Would it be different if the students were not in their classes?

17. Tenure is the permanent right to a position or an office. In teaching, tenure has traditionally been reserved for those who have proven themselves competent in the classroom. Once it is awarded, usually after a provisional term of from two to five or six years, the teacher may not be fired except for gross negligence of duty or some moral offense. The proponents of tenure have maintained that it frees teachers from fears of petty pressures inside or outside the school and enables them to function at their creative best. Recently, however, there seem to be a growing number of opponents of tenure. These people contend that it tempts even the best teachers to relax professionally and stifles creativity. What are the ethical considerations that any full discussion of tenure should address, and why are those considerations important?

18. When faced with the annual decision of how to distribute salary increases to faculty, many administrators elect wherever possible to divide the money among all teachers rather than single out the most deserving ones. (Having everyone a little happy is less troublesome than having a few thrilled and many angry and questioning.) Which action is the more justifiable ethically? Be sure to consider all aspects, including the effects of each action upon the quality of education.

19. Most teacher retirement programs calculate the individual's pension based on the average salary earned during his or her highest earning years. Realizing this, some college presidents routinely promote faculty members the year before their retirement (whether they meet the established requirements for the rank or not). Thus the faculty members can get a slightly higher pension. Is this practice of routine promotion ethical?

20. Is it ethical for students not to work to their capacity? Is it ethical for them to study so diligently that they strain the limits of their physical and emotional endurance? Discuss the various degrees of underwork and overwork that occur among college students and decide in what circumstances each becomes a moral issue.

21. The practice of cheating on homework and examinations is probably as old as education itself. Few would deny that it is an unethical practice in most cases. But what of the dilemma of students who do not cheat on their work but know other students who do? Discuss the moral considerations they should make in deciding whether to inform the teacher. Then decide when they should and when they should not do so.

□ MEDIA AND THE ARTS

1. The scene is a large room at a political convention. The members of a state delegation are entering to caucus about an important issue. The meeting is closed to the public and press. However, one enterprising reporter has anticipated the caucus and is carrying forged credentials identifying her as a member of the delegation. Hoping for a news scoop, she flashes her false credentials at the door, moves inside the room, flips on a concealed tape recorder, and mingles with the crowd. Is she behaving ethically?

2. In 1990 the parents of two young men who committed suicide brought legal action against the rock group Judas Priest. The parents contended that hidden messages ("Do it" and "Let's be dead") in the group's album *Stained Class* caused the men to take their lives. The court held that the rock group bore no legal responsibility, but the moral question remains unanswered. Assuming the alleged messages were hidden in the recording, are the individuals who put them there guilty of a moral offense?

3. In their book *The Early Window: Effects of Television on Children and Youth,* researchers Robert M. Liebert and Joyce Sprafkin cite three detailed reviews of the scholarly literature on violence: Andison's in 1977, Dorr and Kovaric's in 1980, and Hearold's in 1986. (Hearold's review covered 230 separate studies.) All three researchers agree that the effects of violence shown on television are substantial. Specific effects include direct instruction and copying, lowering of inhibitions to aggression, and cultivation and shaping of values.

In addition, Liebert and Sprafkin say the following about a fourth study:

> In a large-scale study conducted for CBS, Belson (1978) collected information about television viewing, aggressive behavior, and other personal characteristics of more than 1,500 male adolescents in London. After equating for a variety of variables related to aggressive behavior, the extent of aggressive behavior of the heavy and light TV viewers was compared. Belson concluded that the evidence "is very strongly supportive of the hypothesis that high exposure to television violence increases the degree to which boys engage in serious violence" (p. 15). (The antisocial behaviors included deeds that were serious enough to be labeled juvenile delinquency such as inflicting bodily harm to others and damage to property.) CBS chose to view the findings as inconclusive, and the study did not receive much publicity. (Just as a note of interest, this study took 8 years to complete and cost CBS $300,000.)[1]

If the author's assertions are accurate, what conclusions do you draw about the morality of showing violence on television? What action, if any, should be taken about violent shows, and by whom?

4a. The essential purpose of advertising is to inform the public that certain goods and services are available. Modern advertising, of course, goes beyond informing and attempts to persuade the public that one product or service is better than all others. And the persuasive tactics that are used are sometimes morally questionable. Examine at least five print ads or commercials and evaluate what is said and implied. Then decide whether each is morally defensible. Detail your findings.

4b. One device increasingly used in modern advertising is the testimonial. An athlete, former politician, or movie/TV star is paid hundreds of thousands of dollars to lend his or her name to a product and become its spokesperson. The celebrity recites someone else's words to praise something he or she may not even use, in order to influence readers or viewers to use the product. Discuss the ethical issues this advertising practice raises.

5. In recent years Hollywood has produced a number of horror films that graphically depict violence. Many of these films force the audience to adopt the perspective of the psychotic killer by filming the action as the killer would see it. All the artistry of special effects departments and new technology, including filming in 3-D, combine to make the stabbings and decapitations more realistic than ever. Discuss the morality of producing and viewing horror films.

6. When advice columnists Ann Landers and Abigail Van Buren were discovered to have recycled old letters (some of them used fifteen years earlier) without notifying their publishers or so labeling the material for their readers, a minor controversy arose. Some readers and newspaper editors believed that the columnists had committed a moral offense, while others disputed that view. What do you think about the morality of such recycling of material?

7. Now that homosexuality is more open and more tolerated in our society, some advertisers are beginning to design advertisements that appeal to a homosexual audience: for example, ads for jeans, whiskey, and cologne. The appeal is often subtle to avoid offending "straight" consumers. Is there anything morally offensive about this advertising practice?

8. There have been reports that the staff of a popular TV show about the investigative work of a government agency is required to submit all scripts to the agency's director for his prior approval. Any scripts that show his agents making a mistake or using questionable tactics in conducting an investigation are allegedly rejected. If these charges are true, is the agency's action ethical? Is the TV staff ethically justified in cooperating?

9. At various times one or more of the major networks have reportedly outlawed certain subjects and treatments: for example, stories about sexually transmitted disease; the portrayal of unmarried couples living together or blacks and whites mingling socially; objective examination of the Vietnam War and the civil rights issue; sympathetic treatment of homosexuals, draft evaders, and militants. Discuss the morality of such censorship.

10. The sponsors of TV shows also can exert influence over the subjects and treatment presented. In some cases they may demand veto power over scripts, reasoning that since they are paying for the show and their product will be identified with it favorably or unfavorably, they should have the final say about its content. Is it morally right for them to demand this veto power?

11. It is common knowledge that most TV commercials have very little appeal to the mind. They aim for the emotions and use our hopes and desires and needs to condition us to buy the products they advertise. Do the writers of TV commercials commit any moral offense by these appeals and devices? Do the sponsors by endorsing them? Do the networks by permitting them to be aired?

12. For a number of years it has been widely recognized that TV has the potential to be the greatest educational device in history. (This includes not just what is presently considered educational TV, but commercial TV as well.) Does the TV industry have any moral obligation to realize that potential? If so, explain the source of that obligation and the kinds of changes in present programming that would be necessary to realize it.

13. TV news reporting calls for careful editing. Thousands of feet of film must be trimmed to fit a tight time schedule. Events that could not be fully covered in hours must be presented in minutes. Without intending to do so, the people who prepare news broadcasts can distort the news and misinform the viewing public. Do TV networks have any special ethical obligation to ensure that such distortion does not occur? If you believe they do, explain why and what kinds of regulations and safeguards would fulfill the obligation.

14. In many newspapers the letters-to-the-editor column is given more than token space and becomes a lively forum for a public discussion of timely issues. The number and relative quality of letters published for or against an issue, and even their arrangement on the page, can subtly influence public opinion. Does this power to influence carry with it any ethical responsibility? If so, what is it and how can it best be met?

15. Newspapers derive part of their income from taking advertisements for, among other things, movies. Occasionally a paper will set standards that must be met by movie ads: for example, the stipulation that the ad contain no prurient appeal. Is it ethical for newspapers to exercise such censorship? If you believe it is, do you think that newspapers that do not censor their ads are behaving unethically?

16. Newspaper columnists very often are given information that amounts to news scoops. They may be given a copy of a letter or memorandum that incriminates a government official or a political aspirant. The dilemma they must face is to decide whether to publish it quickly so that the public can be informed or to delay publication until the information is verified. Do columnists have any ethical obligation? If so, how can it be satisfied?

17. Magazine editors are regularly faced with the difficult job of appraising manuscripts submitted by writers. Often they must consider factors other than the quality of the writing. For example, a well-known writer and a relatively unknown one may submit articles about the same general topic. If the better-known writer's piece is chosen because it is superior, there is no moral issue. Yet sometimes it is chosen even though it is inferior. Under what conditions, if any, would such selection be ethically justifiable?

18. Film studios often buy the movie rights to successful novels. In the process of producing a film, they may make significant changes in plot, characters, and setting. In fact, sometimes the finished film bears little resemblance to the novel. Under what circumstances, if any, is it morally wrong for filmmakers to alter a novel?

19. It is a psychological truism that everything we say and do, every experience we have, helps to shape us favorably or unfavorably. Children in their formative years are especially vulnerable. Yet certain films, because of their story line, require child actors to portray mentally disturbed, criminal, and even savage characters. Is the use of children in such roles ethically acceptable? If you believe that it is sometimes, be sure to specify the conditions that differentiate those situations from unacceptable ones.

20. Is it ethical for an actor or actress to accept a role in a film or TV show if he or she finds its theme morally objectionable?

21. Most colleges today employ media specialists, men and women who prepare audiovisual aids for teachers. Sometimes these people are given assignments that conflict with their principles. For example, they may be directed to produce for a psychology instructor slides and transparencies that mock their religious beliefs. Is it morally acceptable for the media specialists to accept such assignments?

22. Some companies pay movie producers to display their products in films. For example, a soft drink company may pay to have its soda prominently featured, an automobile manufacturer may donate a car with the provision that the hero be shown driving it, and so on. Is there anything morally objectionable about this practice?

□ SEX

1. In many states the law now offers protection against sexual harassment. Moreover, behavior that was formerly considered playful teasing is now considered sexual harassing. For example, a man may make a verbal "pass" at a woman or merely offer what he considers a compliment about the shapeliness of her legs and he may be technically guilty of sexual harassment. Many men believe that a law that makes no distinction between "real offenses" and teasing is unethical. Are they correct?

2. In our culture fornication (sexual intercourse between unmarried men and women) has traditionally been viewed as immoral. The reasons that have supported this judgment have ranged from religious prohibitions to practical considerations, such as the dangers of pregnancy and sexually transmitted disease. The liberalization of religious views, the improvement of birth control techniques, and the development of antibiotics have resulted in a softening of the traditional judgment. The question of the rightness or wrongness of fornication is seldom hotly debated anymore. Yet it remains a debatable issue. Evaluate the morality of fornication in each of the following situations. If the existence of any special conditions in any of the situations would materially change your judgment, specify those conditions and explain how they would change your judgment:

a. Between two 13-year-olds

b. Between two 17-year-olds

c. Between a 25-year-old man and a 21-year-old woman

d. Between a 25-year-old man and a 13-year-old girl

e. Between a 25-year-old woman and a 13-year-old boy

3. Consider this special, though perhaps not altogether uncommon, case of fornication. A 28-year-old man is engaged. About a month before the wedding he meets an old sweetheart with whom he had been intimate. They have dinner together for old times' sake and recall their relationship. By the end of the evening, memory has rekindled passion. They spend the next three days and nights together. Is their fornication ethically justifiable?

4. Some degree of sexual experimentation appears to be a normal part of growing up in our culture. Many teenage boys and girls will indulge in necking and petting (and even intercourse) with partners toward whom they feel only a slight and passing affection. Some, in fact, will on occasion do so with partners they have no feeling for. The sexual activity in such cases is performed not to express love, but to gain experience or to satisfy a biological urge. Is there anything morally questionable about this practice?

5. Sexual promiscuity is frequent indulgence in intercourse with a variety of partners, indiscriminately selected. Is promiscuity immoral? Explain.

6. An unusual case occurred in England some years ago in which a man and his wife were arrested for having sexual intercourse in their yard. Because only a row of flowers separates their yard from their neighbors' and the neighbors' children observed them, the couple was charged with crimes—he with indecent exposure and she with aiding and abetting him. He was found guilty, but she was acquitted after promising not to use the yard for sexual activity again.[1] Was what they did immoral?

7. Like fornication, adultery (sexual intercourse between a man and a woman, either or both of whom is married to someone else) has traditionally been considered immoral. Evaluate the morality of adultery in each of the following cases. If your answer depends on certain conditions, state those conditions.

a. A married woman whose husband was left impotent after an automobile accident has intercourse two or three times a month with a bachelor who works in her office.

b. A man is married to a woman whom he loves but who doesn't meet his sexual needs. Since his job takes him out of town two or three times a month, he uses those occasions to find a woman to supplement his sexual activity.

c. A soldier is fighting overseas for a year. During that time both he and his wife, without telling each other, engage in sexual relations with others.

d. A "liberated" couple joins a mate-swapping club. They attend club parties together, engage in sexual activities with others, then go home together.

e. A married man enjoys a good sexual relationship with his wife but has affairs without her knowledge just to add variety and a sense of adventure to his life.

8. Is it ethically justifiable for a married person to become celibate (for, let us say, religious reasons) without consulting his or her spouse? Is it justifiable to do so if he or she consults the spouse and the spouse refuses to consent?

9. Dr. William Masters and Dr. Virginia Johnson are well known for their research into human sexuality. The method of treatment that they have found effective in treating couples with sexual problems is a two-week vacation "course." The couple checks into a hotel near the clinic and receives instruction in the therapy technique, which consists of proceeding very slowly from just gently embracing each other during the first few days to intercourse later. Though the explanations are provided in the clinic, all physical contact between the couple is reserved for their hotel room. The therapists do not observe the couple.[2] Are these clinics ethically acceptable?

10. The Masters and Johnson clinics have a number of imitators. One of these is a nude encounter group in which men and women with sexual problems meet and learn to perform sexually by experimenting with one another.[3] Is this group ethically acceptable?

11. A number of other sex clinics operate more along the lines of Masters and Johnson but differ in one respect: They use surrogate partners for single patients. That is, if a single man or woman enrolls in the program for treatment, they provide him or her with a sexually skilled partner. (Masters and Johnson used surrogates in their original clinic, but ceased to do so when their use became controversial.) These partners are paid for their services by the clinic.[4] Is the use of surrogate partners ethically acceptable?

12. The problem of crew members' sex drives is a factor in two-month nuclear submarine cruises. It is solved by providing pornography.[5] Is that solution morally acceptable?

13. Legend has it that prostitution is the "world's oldest profession." Some societies have approved it, others have tolerated it, many have tried to eliminate it. Is prostitution immoral in all cases?

14. Our society has traditionally regarded homosexual behavior as a moral abomination. Is it? In answering, comment not only on situations involving consenting adults, but also on those involving a consenting adult and a consenting minor. If your answer differs from your answer on the fornication question, explain why.

15. What are the ethical considerations that arise in cases where people undergo sex-change operations? Are there any situations in which it would not be ethically justifiable to have such an operation?

□ GOVERNMENT

1. Does the federal government have a moral obligation to cover the cost of health care for individuals who cannot afford health insurance or whose health insurance benefits have been exhausted? What about individuals who could have afforded health insurance but gambled that they would not suffer serious illness and who now find themselves unable to afford health care?

2. A businessman has significant holdings in airline stock. He runs for Congress, is elected, and is about to serve on the House Government Activities and Transportation subcommittee, which holds hearings on airline industry issues, such as airline safety. Would it be ethical for him to continue to hold his airline stock?

3. The U.S. government continues to give subsidies to the agricultural industry. Most people have no moral objection to that practice in general. However, many people feel it is morally wrong for the government to give such subsidies to tobacco farmers, whose product is harmful to people's health. Is it morally wrong to subsidize the growing of tobacco?

4. Many people were shocked and angered to learn that the Small Business Administration had made federally guaranteed loans to a pornographic movie theater in Miami Beach and a Times Square sex emporium that features films, peep shows, sexual aids, and pornographic literature.[1] Is there anything morally wrong with a government agency's making loans to such businesses?

5. Just after World War II, when the Allies were prosecuting Nazi war criminals, the U.S. State Department secretly smuggled several hundred Nazi war criminals into the United States, offering them citizenship and jobs in exchange for Soviet intelligence information. The State Department's action contravened the orders of President Roosevelt and President Truman. For decades after the illegal operation took place, relevant files were withheld from Congress, the courts, and the CIA. Only the FBI and military intelligence officers knew of the operation.[2] Is it possible that the smuggling and subsequent cover-up were ethical despite their illegality?

6. At present it is against the law for teachers to lead students in prayer in U.S. public schools. However, a growing number of citizens believe that the law should be changed. Discuss the ethical implications of this controversy.

7. Does the United States, as a democratic nation, have any moral obligation to accept immigrants from poor, underdeveloped countries? Does it have any obligation to grant political asylum to defectors from totalitarian regimes?

8. As a result of the ABSCAM probe of political corruption, a number of representatives and one senator were convicted of accepting bribes for political favors. Many people believe that, though the senator and representatives' behavior was indefensible, the ABSCAM operation itself was morally offensive. The basis of their objection is that FBI agents posed as Arab sheiks and tempted the senator and representatives with bribes for illegal favors. Is such an operation ever justifiable?

9. Political campaigns frequently raise the dilemma of to what extent a person is justified in tolerating evil to achieve a good end. A senatorial candidate, for example, may find his staff attacking his opponent with slogans and emotional appeals unrelated to any campaign issue. Is there anything morally offensive in his allowing such methods to continue? If so, are there any special circumstances in which their use would be justified?

10. In order to gain information to help in the election campaign, members of a political party may infiltrate the opposing party. Pretending acceptance of the opposing party's philosophy and the desire to serve, they may attend the convention and try to get as close as possible to the decision makers, in person or with electronic devices, so that they can inform their own party leaders. Comment on the morality of this practice.

11. The ancient military saying "To the victor belong the spoils" is traditionally applied in politics. A large number of government jobs—at the local and state as at the national level—are appointive. Every time one party is voted out and another voted in, the old appointees step aside and new ones are named, usually from among the ranks of the hardworking party faithful. Examine this practice in light of the principles we have been using.

12. Modern political campaigns are expensive, the costs frequently running into the millions of dollars. Since the contributions of individuals are seldom sufficient to meet this expense, political action committees (PACs) representing special interest groups often make sizeable donations to candidates for state and federal offices. If elected, candidates may feel obligated to endorse legislation that benefits groups that supported them and oppose legislation that does not benefit them. Discuss the reasonableness of this feeling in light of the principles we have been using.

13. Some states have rules forbidding all executive and legislative employees to have an interest in business activity that could conflict with their public service, to personally hold any investment in an enterprise about which they might be making decisions as government officials, and to communicate to others any confidential information that would help them gain a business or professional advantage. Are such rules ethically sound? Show how the principles we have been using support or challenge such rules.

14. Elected officials are sometimes offered special considerations. They may, for instance, be given preferential treatment in obtaining travel accommodations and reductions in fare. When they take a vacation, the hotels and restaurants they visit may discount their bills. Is it morally wrong for them to accept such considerations? Why or why not?

15. Lobbying is a political institution almost as old as government itself. It is the advocacy of a particular interest group's viewpoint, usually by paid employees. Such employees, lobbyists, are registered with the government. Their job is to bring the interests of their employers to the attention of the lawmakers, informing them of which bills have the support of their people and which do not, encouraging the lawmaker to write special legislation, and even suggesting the specific details such legislation might include. Is it ethical to allow lobbying to take place? In what ways and to what extent is it ethically acceptable for legislators to be influenced by lobbyists?

16. Do rich nations have any obligation to help poor nations? If so, in what way and to what extent?

17. Whether or not they have an obligation to help poor nations, rich nations often do help. But sometimes they attach conditions to their aid; that is, they demand the privilege of influencing the poor nation's government or they expect support for their international policies of trade. Is it ethical for rich nations to attach such conditions to their aid?

18. Pollution is threatening our natural resources. Every responsible person wants to protect our planet for the future. Yet some irresponsible people care only for the profit or pleasure of the moment. Does the government have any moral obligation to eliminate pollution? If so, identify some ways in which it might fulfill that obligation. (Be sure not to gloss over any moral dilemmas that those ways would cause.)

19. Most countries that have tried to deal with the problem of overpopulation have found that one of the most difficult tasks is to educate the poor to use birth control techniques according to directions (for example, to take birth control pills each day rather than skip several days). Some of these countries have found it much simpler and more effective to run campaigns urging men and women to submit to sterilization operations. At least one country gave a free transistor radio to anyone who was sterilized. Are such campaigns ethical? Is it morally right for governments to become involved in population control at all?

20. According to the Anti-Slavery Society for the Protection of Human Rights, "slavery, serfdom, debt bondage, the sale of children, and servile forms of marriage" exist in at least thirty-eight countries in Asia, Africa, and Latin America.[3] Presumably the United States enjoys diplomatic relations and trade with some of these countries. Does the United States have any moral obligation to do something about these practices? If so, what?

21. The ideological differences that have existed among the major world powers for the past several decades have made spying among countries almost inevitable. Though the extent to which the United States practices spying is understandably not easy to ascertain, it seems certain that the Central Intelligence Agency is involved in such work in numerous countries around the world. In what circumstances, if any, and to what extent is its spying morally permissible?

22. In its efforts to maintain national security, the Federal Bureau of Investigation has used informants, men and women who make accusations against others or provide the information that supports such accusations. In some cases, informants step forward to assist the FBI in advance and are directed what to learn and how they might go about learning it. In such cases, this question often arises: "How far is it ethically permissible for an investigative agency to go in contributing to illegal activities in order to gain evidence to prosecute lawbreakers?" For example, would it be permissible for the agency to provide (through the informant) the guns, explosives, and vehicles needed to commit the crime? Would it be right for the agency to permit or encourage the informant to provoke the criminals to commit a more serious crime than they had intended?

23. Some years ago the tomb of an ancient Chinese noblewoman was discovered near the city of Changsha. The remarkable condition of the body, the clothes, and the ornaments of the tomb recalled the greatness of the dynasty to which she belonged, the Han dynasty that ruled from about 200 B.C. to A.D. 200. Under these rulers, within a single generation wars among numerous territories were quelled; all of what is now China was united under one economic system, one political philosophy, one legal system; roads were built and agricultural reforms introduced. As a result of these stabilizing social changes, the arts and crafts flourished as never before. Yet all these reforms were not introduced democratically; they were forced on the people, often tyrannically. Dissent was not tolerated.[4] Did the positive consequences that resulted justify the methods used to achieve them? Would tyranny today be morally acceptable if there were a guarantee that it would achieve good?

24. The North American continent was "discovered," claimed for various countries, and later colonized and developed into the nations of Mexico, the United States, and Canada. However, at the time of the various discoveries, there were already people living on the continent. Discuss the morality of the process by which the continent was claimed and colonized.

25. In recent years there has been growing concern about the safety of nuclear power plants. At the same time continuing energy shortages have increased pressure for the building of more of these plants. Should the government approve further building? Do present regulations and restrictions meet the moral demands of the situation? If not, how should present regulations and restrictions be modified?

26. Is the concept of private property ethically justifiable in a world where there is widespread proverty? Why or why not?

□ LAW

1. A California Superior Court judge ordered a Sacramento woman to stop smoking in front of her 5-year-old son. The decision came during a custody dispute. The boy's father claimed that breathing secondhand smoke could harm the boy's health. Does morality support the judge's ruling?

2. Is police brutality ever justifiable? If so, in what circumstances?

3. Is it ethical to punish criminals for crimes they committed while temporarily insane? Is it ethical to punish criminals who were severely retarded and didn't understand the gravity of their crime?

4. If a man kills his wife, who was six months pregnant, and the fetus does not survive, should he be charged with one count of murder or two?

5. Often the penalty for white-collar crime is considerably less than for street crime. Someone who makes millions of dollars in illegal insider trading in stocks, for example, will spend less time in jail than someone who steals a car. Moreover, he will serve his time in a comparatively comfortable facility. Is this difference in punishment morally justifiable?

6. Early in a famous court case, a woman juror is approached by a publisher with a book contract if she will agree to record her experiences on the jury. The publisher envisions a book that tells what was said in the jury room, who argued what, and how the men and women of the jury came to their final decision. Would it be ethical for her to accept the contract?

7. Some years ago an American Indian group occupied some public land in the Black Hills National Forest in South Dakota. They claimed the area was a holy land to them: their birthplace, the graveyard of their ancestors, and the center of their universe. For this reason, they said the area should be turned into a permanent, religion-based Indian community. The government argued that the Indians have no legal right to the land; the Indians argued that they have both a legal and a moral right. Do you agree that the Indians have a moral right?

8. A number of law enforcement agencies are now using a hand-held device called a Taser gun to deal with violent-crime suspects and unruly prison inmates. The flashlight-sized device shoots darts connected to wires to deliver a 50,000-volt shock. (Reportedly the device produces no after-effects.)[1] Discuss the conditions, if any, under which the Taser gun's use would be morally acceptable.

9. Alan Dershowitz, Harvard law professor and successful criminal lawyer, has written these words about his defense of people accused of violent crimes: "I do not apologize for (or feel guilty about) helping to let a murderer go free—even though I realize that someday one of my clients may go out and kill again. . . . I am proud to be regarded as overzealous on behalf of my clients."[2] Is this view ethically sound? Is it moral for a lawyer to offer a vigorous defense for those who admit (at least in private) that they are guilty of the crimes for which they are charged?

10. In recent years there have been numerous expressions of public outrage over the parole of people convicted of violent crimes. Discuss the ethical considerations in the issue of parole and decide what direction they suggest for lawmakers.

11. In many colleges across the nation, students are required to pay an activity fee that supports cultural, entertainment, and sports programs.

Apparently in most cases the student bodies of the colleges originally approved of the idea, and from all indications the majority of students do not object to paying the fee because the student government decides how the funds are to be used. However, in at least one state, legislators have challenged the idea. Presumably acting on behalf of the minority of students who oppose the fee, a group of New York state legislators introduced a bill some years ago that would forbid any college in the state university system from charging a student activity fee. (The bill was defeated.) Is it ethical for a university to require students to pay such a fee? Does a legislature have the moral right to forbid a university to do so?

12. Some states still have laws on the books that make fornication, sodomy, and even the practice of contraception by married couples a crime. These laws are seldom applied, and the climate of opinion today would surely support their repeal. Yet when they were written it was taken for granted that the state had the moral right, and even the obligation, to make laws about such matters. Evaluate that view, using the appropriate ethical principles.

13. Laws concerning statutory rape are not only still in existence but are often still applied. (Statutory rape, unlike rape, need not involve the element of force. Any act of intercourse between a minor and an adult is a statutory offense because a minor is held to be incapable of giving consent. The definition of minor, of course, varies from state to state.) Are such laws ethically sound?

14. The job of the police is to protect the health, safety, and welfare of the general public. To meet this responsibility they must obviously not only prevent any activity that threatens the public, but also anticipate such activity before it actually threatens. Many police officials believe that this latter responsibility is moral justification for maintaining close surveillance on political action groups and for dispersing large groups of people listening to inflammatory political speeches. Others disagree, claiming that this line of reasoning leads to the denial of the constitutional rights of free speech and free assembly and to the establishment of a police state. Which position is more in keeping with the ethical principles developed in the earlier part of this book? Explain.

15. Prostitution is illegal in most parts of the United States. Yet, unlike other crimes, it has no victim. Two people freely choose to have sexual contact and to treat that contact as a business transaction. Is it ethical for society to legislate against a victimless act? (The term *victim* is used here in the legal sense. In a different sense, the emotional and perhaps the moral, it could be argued that both participants are victims.)

16. Is it ever morally permissible for the state to take children away from their natural parents and place them in orphanages or with foster parents? In answering, consider situations in which the parents are alcoholics or drug addicts or neglect or abuse their children.

17. Capital punishment is the taking of a criminal's life in punishment for his or her crimes. Throughout history it has been supported by most societies, often even for crimes we would consider minor. During this century, however, more and more people in Europe and America have come to regard it as morally intolerable, even in the case of heinous crimes. Do you agree? Explain.

18. Due to the increase in crime and the inability of the courts to process cases, a practice known as plea bargaining has developed in large metropolitan areas. It consists of the defense attorney's making a deal with the prosecution—if the prosecution agrees to reduce the charge against the defendant, the defendant will plead guilty and waive his or her right to a jury trial. Plea bargaining appeals to criminals because it allows them to be tried for a lesser crime than they committed. It appeals to prosecutors because it spares them keeping track of witnesses for months and even years. It appeals to judges because it expedites their handling of cases. Evaluate the morality of plea bargaining.

19. In civil lawsuits it is an established practice for attorneys to charge "contingency fees," in other words, to have their clients agree in advance to pay them a percentage of their settlement award. In many cases these fees are as high as 50 percent. Evaluate the morality of contingency fees.

20. Is it ethical for attorneys to base their fees on their clients' ability to pay; that is, to charge a rich person much more than a poor person for the same services? Explain your position.

21. The ideal of justice demands that every person charged with a crime receive equal legal representation regardless of race, creed, nationality, or financial status. However, in practice, minority groups and the poor receive second-class representation at best. Does the legal profession have any moral obligation to strive to realize the ideal? If so, in what ways might it honor that obligation?

22. There is a controversy today over what kinds of conditions society ought to provide in prisons. Advocates of improved conditions suggest that society has been vengeful in its practices, seeking more to punish than to rehabilitate. They call for more humane conditions, conditions consistent with the human dignity of the inmates. On the other hand, many criticize this thinking as too permissive. Prison should be a drab, monotonous, unpleasant experience, they reason, or it will not deter criminals from repeating their crimes. Discuss the ethical considerations that must be faced in any full discussion of prison conditions.

23. A young woman removed her bathing suit on a public beach. Many people gathered around her, some to take pictures, others to scold her. Then someone called the police. They arrested her and charged her with "public lewdness." The young woman believed the law violated her rights. Do you agree? Is a law that, in effect, forces people to wear clothes in public unethical?

24. Many urban police departments use undercover policewomen to arrest men who do business with prostitutes. The policewomen dress like prostitutes and walk up and down streets where prostitutes are known to work. When unsuspecting men approach the policewomen and proposition them, they are arrested. Is it ethically defensible for police to use such tactics?

25. The most controversial moral issue of our time may well be the issue of abortion. The Supreme Court's liberal ruling has not diminished the vigor of debate. The very mention of the issue can trigger emotional outbursts. Most people tend to gravitate toward polar attitudes: "Anything less than abortion on demand is a denial of the most basic right of women," or "Any form of abortion at any stage of pregnancy is premeditated murder." In taking such positions they close their minds to the complexities of the issue and miss the many distinctions that must be made. Any meaningful discussion of abortion must address itself to at least these fundamental questions: Does a woman have absolute rights over her body or are there limitations on those rights? When does life begin? At what stage of prenatal development, if any, is the fetus properly regarded as a person? (This question is a crucial one in the law, since at the moment a person is present the issue of civil rights arises.) Are there sufficient differences among the various kinds of abortion cases to call for different moral judgments? For example, is the case of the 14-year-old victim of rape different from that of the wealthy, childless society matron? Are either of those cases different from that of the poor woman who already has ten children or from that of the young married working woman? Discuss the morality of abortion.

□ BUSINESS

1. A group of hemophiliacs who have contracted AIDS is charging that the manufacturer of the blood clotting product that infected them knew there was a chance that some of the blood was contaminated with the hepatitis virus. The group further charges that the manufacturer had available a process that would have purified the product, yet chose for economic reasons not to use the process on the product or to discard the tainted supply already on hand. The AIDS virus had not been identified when the company made its alleged decision; however, it is now known that the purification process would have killed the AIDS virus as well as the hepatitis virus. Did the company behave morally? Discuss the degree, if any, of their culpability.[1]

2. Some years ago the Campbell Soup Company wanted to feature in advertisements a picture showing the solid ingredients in its soup. Unfortunately, the advertising group found that the solid ingredients sank to the bottom and were barely visible. All that could be seen was the broth. Then they hit upon a solution—they put marbles in the bottom of the bowl before pouring in any soup. Thus the vegetables sat nicely on the top, giving the appearance of thick soup. Discuss the morality of this solution.

3. The idea of equal pay for equal work is generally accepted as morally sound. But are there situations in which the application of this idea would be immoral? Why or why not?

4. Because products tend to become obsolete much faster today than they did thirty or forty years ago, research and development is one of the most important activities in modern business. However, it is an expensive activity. Some companies try to save money by paying people to conduct corporate espionage; that is, to spy on competitors' research and development operations. Is such espionage ever morally justifiable?

5. Is it ethical for grocery store produce departments to package one overripe tomato and one underripe one in every three- or six-pack of tomatoes? Is it ethical for meat departments to turn the better side up when packaging meat?

6. Is it ethical for companies to require employees to take a polygraph test before they are promoted? Would your answer be different in the case of a company whose products are made from a secret formula that competitors have so far been unsuccessful in imitating?

7. Is it ethical for liquor companies to create ads linking the consumption of liquor with friendship, popularity, love, and financial success? Would your answer change if the liquor company created an occasional public service ad that stressed the need for responsibility in drinking?

8. In the Middle Ages, the seller was considered responsible for defects in merchandise. Today, though the courts may give relief to a buyer if the defects are glaring, the basic rule is "Let the buyer beware." Is this rule more ethically defensible than the medieval rule?

9. Is it morally acceptable for employers to screen employees for AIDS? For company health insurance carriers to drop the coverage of anyone who tests HIV-positive on a company AIDS test?

10. An evening news co-anchorwoman at WBZ-TV in Boston decided she wanted a child even though she was unmarried. When she became pregnant, several newspaper reporters and columnists criticized her. One said she and other single mothers "thumb their noses at the old social and moral conventions." Several local clergymen said her high visibility on TV would make her decision seem like an endorsement of unwed parenthood, an inappropriate message to send to young people. The station management disagreed and stood behind her decision. Were they on solid moral grounds in doing so?

11. The Reagan administration once proposed that an existing ban on exports of unapproved drugs and pharmaceuticals be repealed, thus permitting American drug companies to sell abroad drugs that have been banned (or have not yet been approved) by the Food and Drug Administration. The justification offered for the proposal was that it would help the U.S. balance of trade and be beneficial to individual companies.[2] Is such a proposal morally defensible?

12. A decade ago, nineteen people, most of them employees of two Japanese electronics firms, were charged with scheming to steal computer secrets from IBM.[3] Such activity is a legal offense, but many business-people believe there is nothing morally wrong with it, that it is necessary in today's fast-changing, competitive business world. Discuss the morality of this practice.

13. Sometimes a new invention is viewed as a threat by an industry. For example, if an efficient steam engine were developed for automobiles, the oil industry could anticipate a ruinous decline in gasoline sales. In such cases the industry might be tempted to buy all rights to the invention in order to prevent it from being marketed. Would such a purchase be moral in any circumstances? Explain.

14. In business ventures timing can often make the difference between success and failure. Occasionally, timing can pose a dilemma for executives. For example, the officers of a company may be formally obligated to consult their stockholders on certain types of policy decisions. Yet situations may arise in which there is no time to consult them. In such situations there is a good chance for the company to profit but with some risk of loss. Under what conditions, if any, would it be proper for the executives to act without consulting?

15. Drug manufacturers are required to conduct tests on new drugs for a full year to be sure that there are no dangerous side effects. One relatively small company has had a promising new antibiotic in testing for eight months. There have been no indications of any harmful effects. Now the company learns that a large competitor is about to market a similar drug. It concludes that with a four-month advantage, the competitor will control the market. The small company will be driven out of business. It decides to change the dates on its research and add four months of fake test results so that the antibiotic may be marketed immediately. Discuss the morality of this decision.

16. Barbiturate and amphetamine addiction continues to give cause for national concern. Each year hundreds of thousands of pills manage to slip into the black market and are sold illegally, often to young people. Some observers, including the head of a congressional crime committee that spent two years probing the problem of illegal drug trafficking,[4] believe that the drug manufacturers cannot be blamed if their products are put to illegitimate use. Do drug manufacturers have any moral responsibility to ensure that their products are not put to such use?

17. It is fairly common today to read of professional athletes refusing to sign contracts with their teams until they are given higher salaries. These demands, which can be for millions of dollars, are regarded by team owners as a form of blackmail. The players, however, believe that their skills are a saleable commodity and that they are justified in getting as high a salary as they can bargain for. Are such demands justifiable? Are they only so in certain circumstances? Explain.

18. In the early days of the labor union movement, workers were often treated unfairly. Working hours and conditions were injurious to their health, wages were unfairly low, and fringe benefits were nonexistent. Today the situation is different. Some unions have achieved most of their reasonable demands. However, because of the pressure to keep winning new benefits, they make ever more extravagant demands and use the threat of strikes to gain them. Do union demands ever become an unethical use of power? If so, in what circumstances?

19. Strip-mining is the digging of shallow deposits of coal. It has been shown to ruin the land for all agricultural use. Recent experiments in reclaiming strip-mined land (for example, by dumping sewage on it) have shown signs of promise. But there is still no certain reclaiming technique. Is strip-mining ethical?

20. Investment brokers sometimes have a few clients who live hundreds of miles from their offices. For example, a Wall Street broker may provide investment counseling for his hometown relatives in upstate New York. By arranging to see them during his vacation visits home, he can claim his plane fare or car rental fees and perhaps even many of his meals as business expenses. In other words, he can deduct them on his tax return or, if he is employed by a company, claim them on his expense account. Is this practice ethical?

21. In some businesses—for example, advertising—executives are relatively mobile, changing jobs with unusual frequency. Executives planning such a change can increase their worth to their new employer by taking their clients with them; that is, by meeting with their clients before leaving the company and encouraging them to switch their business to the new company. Discuss the ethical considerations of this practice.

22. Certain hotels do a good share of their business in "hot bed" rentals— the rental of rooms by the hour for purposes of prostitution. Such hotels do not employ the prostitutes or have any direct connection with their trade. They merely allow the prostitutes to check into a hotel room many times a night, each time with a different partner. Is it moral for hotels to permit this use of their premises? Is it moral for a hotel clerk to work in a hotel in which this practice is allowed?

23. Restaurateurs may be strongly tempted to increase their profits by buying old, chemically preserved meat at discount prices or by reheating the same food several days in a row. Discuss the morality of such practices.

24. Heavy-construction companies must usually engage in competitive bidding for their contracts. This practice demands that they anticipate every material and labor cost months and even years ahead and commit themselves to complete a project for a specified amount of money. A mistake in calculating or a failure to anticipate a significant increase in prices can bankrupt a company. Is it ever ethical for a construction company to use materials that are substandard in order to offset such errors or increased expenses and thereby remain solvent?

25. Employees' worth to their employers may diminish before they are eligible for retirement. In such cases the employer is faced with the dilemma of choosing between retaining an old and trusted yet unproductive worker for five or ten more years, or firing that worker and jeopardizing his or her retirement. Does an employer have a moral obligation to such employees? In discussing this, be sure to mention any special circumstances that would alter your judgment.

26. As the costs of running a business increase every year, efficiency is more and more the byword of the successful business person. The axioms of the efficiency expert are "Eliminate what need not be done; simplify what must be done; combine tasks wherever possible." Putting these axioms into practice means, of course, eliminating people's jobs. Under what circumstances is it moral to do so?

27. Book publishers are always in search of a best-seller. When they find a manuscript that they feel has the requisite qualities for success, they try to offer the author the most attractive contractual terms they can in order to induce him or her to sign with their company. Sometimes they will realize that a competitor is in a better position to market the book than they are and that the author would therefore do better to sign with the competitor. Is it ethical for them to withhold that information from the author?

28. Living in a neighborhood where a house of prostitution flourishes upsets many people, especially those with children. In cases where the house is rented, a group of local citizens may band together and pressure the landlord to evict the prostitutes. Is it morally acceptable for them to do this?

29. Employers have expressed concern about job candidates' lying on résumés and job applications. Consequently, some companies are requiring all job applicants to take a lie detector test as part of the initial job screening process. Is such a practice ever ethically justifiable? If so, under what conditions? Is a job applicant ethically responsible for truthfully answering all questions asked by a prospective employer?

30. A manufacturer received a multimillion-dollar contract to supply vehicles for a city transportation system. The vehicles proved to have a number of major defects that endangered the safety of the riders. When city officials sued the manufacturer, an investigation was started. An employee of the manufacturer voluntarily testified that his company deliberately used substandard workmanship, practices, and materials. The employee was fired for giving out confidential information. Was the action by the company justifiable?

31. To guard against the destruction of their crops by pests, farmers often spray their crops with pesticides that may be harmful to humans. Discuss the morality of this practice.

32. Careless mining and timber harvesting in tropical forests can destroy entire species of flora and fauna, create soil problems, and even threaten the existence of primitive people who are reliant on what the forests provide. Yet in a number of countries business entrepreneurs are exploiting the rain forests for profit. Under what conditions, if any, is it ethical for a mining or lumber company to harvest the resources of a rain forest?

□ MEDICINE

1. A doctor allegedly took one couple's frozen embryo and gave it to another couple. The embryo was subsequently implanted and in nine months the child was born. Then the donor couple learned what the doctor had done and filed a lawsuit. Did the doctor behave unethically? If so, exactly what offense was he guilty of?[1]

2. Dr. Jack Kevorkian (also called "Dr. Death") has achieved notoriety by assisting terminally ill people in committing suicide. He provides them with a specially designed machine that allows them to push a button and release a fatal dose of anesthesia into their bloodstream. Kevorkian believes that what he does is not immoral. In fact, he speaks of the "goodness of planned death" and dismisses criticisms of him as "emotionalism." Discuss the ethical questions surrounding Kevorkian's medical "specialty."

3. In testing a patient's blood, a doctor learns that the patient has AIDS. He tells the patient, who says, "I don't want my wife to know I have the disease." Should the doctor honor the patient's request, or should he tell the wife?

4. Some years ago surgeons in Mexico City successfully grafted tissue from a miscarried fetus into the brains of two Parkinson's disease victims, and the victims showed dramatic improvement. Researchers speculate that Alzheimer's disease victims may also be similarly treated. This breakthrough raises a question about the use of aborted fetuses. Is it morally acceptable to use fetal tissue in this way? Would it be morally acceptable for a woman to get pregnant just for the purpose of having an abortion and selling the fetus to medical research institutes?

5. John L. Lacey of Savannah, Georgia, accidentally spilled paint solvent on himself and it ignited, burning every part of his body except the top of his head and the soles of his feet. Despite his critical condition, about thirty medical centers around the country refused to treat him because he lacked medical insurance. (Baltimore City Hospital finally accepted him after the governor of Georgia promised financial aid.)[2] Discuss the morality of the hospitals' refusal to treat Lacey.

6. Some medical clinics participate in the testing of drugs that are still in the experimental stage. In such situations the Food and Drug Administration stipulates that the physician must explain to the patient the nature of the drug, its possible benefits, and the element of risk in using it. In certain situations, however, physicians may decide not to provide those explanations. The number of their patients may be so large that they feel they cannot spare the time to do so, or their patients may be generally uneducated and therefore likely to be confused by details. Does either of these reasons justify a physician's withholding explanation? Can you think of any other reason that would?

7. Is it ever morally justifiable to use orphans for medical research? For example, would it be justifiable to catheterize the urinary tracts of infants in an orphanage for a study of bacteria present in healthy individuals? (Such an experiment would pose no danger to the infants.)

8. Though outlawed in some states, the practice of fee-splitting is widespread in medicine. It consists of a physician, usually a doctor of internal medicine, referring patients to a particular surgeon and the surgeon's sharing part of his or her fee with the referring physician. Is this practice ethically acceptable?

9. Some hospitals are publicly financed and controlled. Others are run by private individuals or corporations and operated on a profit-making basis. The latter, by their nature, are run with an emphasis on efficiency and a profit margin calculated in the charges for room, medication, and surgical costs. Is it ethical for hospitals to be profit-making?

10. In some cases expensive medical treatments are necessary to maintain life yet are out of the average person's financial reach. An example is the use of a dialysis machine. To pay for such treatment people must wipe out their savings and even mortgage their homes and valuables. To qualify for state aid, they must in effect be prepared to take a pauper's oath. Such a situation is obviously tragic. Is it also unethical in any way? Explain.

11. The choice of who should be given priority in the use of a rare and expensive machine like the dialysis machine can be an agonizing one. Very often it is a life-or-death decision for the many patients whose existence depends on it. Make a list of the most important considerations that should be made in reaching such a decision, and comment on the relative importance of each.

12. Some countries, notably Great Britain, have initiated maintenance programs for drug addicts. Merely by signing up, an addict becomes entitled to free drugs in doses sufficient to stabilize and maintain his or her habit. Such programs reduce the incidence of drug-related crimes and facilitate research into the phenomenon of addiction. Some critics, however, claim that these programs are immoral because they approve and support physically and emotionally harmful behavior. Is this criticism ethically valid?

13. Members of the Jehovah's Witnesses religious sect believe that blood transfusion is sinful. If they or their children suffer a serious accident and lose enough blood to require transfusion, they must in conscience refuse it. This poses a dilemma for attending physicians. Consider the following cases and decide whether the physician should or should not administer the transfusion. (In each case, the patient is not likely to survive without transfusion.)

a. The patient is an adult and, while conscious, demands that she not receive blood.

b. The patient is an adult, but is unconscious; his wife states that were he conscious he would not accept blood.

c. The patient is a child; he is unconscious; his parents refuse to sign the permission form.

14. For a long time in Western civilization, autopsy was regarded as an immoral practice that profaned the dead. As a result of this view, there was no legal way for medical school professors and students to obtain corpses. Dedicated to their art, they frequently either dug up recently buried corpses or paid others to do so, without the consent of the dead person's relatives. Were it not for this ghoulish practice, medical science would surely not have developed nearly so extensively or rapidly as it has. Was the practice ethically justifiable?

15. Psychologists and psychiatrists often deal with cases of impotence. As part of their treatment of unmarried patients, they may prescribe a visit to a prostitute. This practice is illegal in most states. Is it also immoral?

16. About one baby out of every six hundred born in the United States has Down's syndrome. Such children have slanted eyes, broad noses, and IQs of about 30. Many are born with fatal physical defects: Parts of vital organs may be missing, the intestines may be blocked, or the heart may not function properly. Often surgery is necessary if they are to survive beyond the first few days of life. The parents must face the question of whether to permit such surgery and save the child, which would mean spending thousands of dollars for special care and education (and in some cases, for institutionalization), or whether to withhold permission and let the child die. Anthony Shaw, an associate professor of surgery and pediatrics at the University of Virginia Medical Center, cites the conflicting views of surgeons over the morality of withholding permission.[3] One is that, in any such situation, not operating would be tantamount to murder. Another is that operating would be wrong because "the emotional and financial costs involved are too great to justify the procedure." The third view, Shaw's own, is more flexible. He believes that the circumstances, which can be fully evaluated only by the parents, may make operation right in one case but wrong in another. Which position is most ethically sound and why?

17. Serious accidents can leave their victims comatose for months and even years. The longer the coma lasts, the less chance the person has of regaining consciousness. There are people who live in that state, cared for at considerable expense in hospitals or nursing homes, unable to relate to their loved ones, unaware that they are technically alive. Such cases inevitably raise the question of euthanasia (mercy killing). Merely by injecting a poisonous substance into a vein, a doctor or nurse could spare the victims their limbo of near-life and grant them a painless death. Would it be ethically justifiable to do so in such a situation? Would it be justifiable in any other situation?

18. The development of organ-transplant techniques has increased the need for donors. Since organs such as the heart can only be (ethically) removed from persons who have just died, the age-old question "When does death occur?" has taken on new importance. Some medical authorities say it occurs when the heart has stopped beating and fails to respond to massage or chemical stimulants. Others say death occurs when the central nervous system has ceased to function (that is, when reflexes cannot be aroused). One authority, Hans Jonas, however, reasons as follows: *"Since we do not know the exact borderline between life and death,* nothing less than the maximum definition of death will do—brain death plus heart death plus any other indication that may be pertinent—before final violence [for example, the taking of an organ for transplant purposes] is allowed to be done."[4] Keeping in mind that Jonas's conclusion would reduce the number of transplant donors, evaluate his reasoning in light of the principles in this book.

19. According to at least one authority, a number of doctors around the country are prescribing amphetamines rather freely for their patients. Is this practice ethical? In answering, consider that amphetamines are habit-forming and can produce symptoms of schizophrenia and paranoia.[5]

20. Hospital workers in a large urban area feel that they are not being paid enough and that their fringe benefits are substandard. They decide to strike. Taking advantage of the special need for their services during holiday periods, they plan the strike to take place ten days before a major holiday weekend. This timing, they expect, will pressure hospital management to meet their demands. Discuss the morality of this strike.

□ SCIENCE

1. Medical research has proven that secondhand smoke—that which is inhaled by nonsmokers in the company of smokers—causes lung disease, including cancer. What are the moral implications of this finding for parents? What are they for businesspeople such as restaurant owners?

2. Some people believe that no warm-blooded animal should ever be used in laboratory experiments that cause them pain. Others say the use of animals is legitimate only in research to cure serious diseases. What is the most ethical response to this controversial issue?

3. The site of an old Cherokee Indian Village in Tennessee was about to be flooded in the process of creating a new Tennessee Valley Authority dam. In an effort to find and preserve the artifacts of Indian civilization known to be buried in the area, archaeologists from a University of Tennessee museum undertook extensive digging. The Cherokee Indians objected to the dam because it represented "flooding a whole race of people's history and heritage off the map." They also objected to the digging because in their view it desecrated the graves of their ancestors.[1] Evaluate the morality both of the government's building the dam and of the archaeological team's digging the area.

4. Some years ago a study was made to determine the psychological effects of oral contraceptives. About four hundred poor women, who had sought family planning assistance, participated. Most of the women were Mexican Americans with large families. Some of the women were given oral contraceptives; others were given dummy pills with no birth control chemical. As a result, six of the women in the "dummy group" became pregnant.[2] Evaluate the ethical character of the study.

5. It is now possible for a woman whose husband is sterile to be artificially inseminated with the semen of a donor. Is this practice ethical? If it is in some circumstances but not in others, be sure to explain those circumstances carefully.

6. It is now possible for a woman whose ovaries cannot produce an ovum to receive one from a donor. Is this practice ethical? If so, under what conditions?

7. A businesswoman wants to have a baby but can't spare the nine months. She goes to a laboratory and, following a new scientific technique, "conceives" a baby from her ovum and her husband's sperm. Then she has the fertilized egg implanted in another woman's uterus. Nine months later, the baby safely delivered, she pays the woman for her "labor." Comment on the morality of this procedure.

8. Much of what we hear about the advent of test-tube babies still has the ring of science fiction to it. Yet in all probability a successful technique for conceiving and nurturing a human fetus in an artificial uterus is certain to be developed. Naturally such an achievement will be preceded by many fumbling, partially successful efforts. Many scientists, in other words, will be creating human embryos, sustaining them for a time—for a few days at first, and then as their techniques become refined, for a few weeks, three months, seven months. Most, perhaps all, of these embryos and fetuses will be destroyed when they have served their scientific purpose. Is such creation of fetuses ethical? Is their destruction ethical?

9. A scientific organization wishes to conduct research on the effects of ultrasound on human beings. It secures the permission of a local hospital to bombard fetuses that are about to be legally aborted and then to autopsy them after abortion. Is such an experiment ethical?

10. A famous experiment by Yale University's Dr. Jose Delgado dramatized the effectiveness of electrical stimulation of the brain (ESB) as a means of controlling behavior. He "wired" the brain of a fighting bull and demonstrated that merely by pushing a button and sending an electrical current coursing into the animal's brain, he could stop it in the middle of an enraged charge. He also showed that repeated stimulation diminished the bull's natural aggressiveness. Similar experiments have shown that the same effects occur in humans. For example, people given to uncontrollable fits of rage can have their brains so wired that, when they feel a seizure coming on, they need only press a button to be instantly calmed. Is the wiring operation ethical if the patient consents to it? Are there any circumstances in which it would be ethical even if he or she did not consent?

11. Another area of research that shows potential for control of behavior is chemical stimulation of the brain (CSB). Tiny tubes can be placed in strategic parts of the brain and chemicals secreted on a timed-release basis. A given emotional state can thus be maintained in the patient independent of his or her control. Following are some of the uses CSB might be put to. Examine the morality of each:

> **a.** Candidates for high public office or for appointive positions such as the president's cabinet could be required to submit to CSB so that the public could be assured no conscious or subconscious aggressiveness in its officials would lead the country into war.

> **b.** Persons convicted of violent crimes could be treated to ensure that they would not act violently again.

> **c.** Students who have very short attention spans that hamper their learning or who have negative attitudes toward teachers and the learning process could be treated to increase their learning potential.

> **d.** Newborn children could be treated so that they would not be susceptible to propaganda or to the promptings of fanatics.

12. Throughout history it has been the practice in many countries to use convicts in scientific experiments. The practice continues today. If, for example, researchers develop a chemical that preliminary exploratory work indicates will cure a fatal disease, they may seek volunteers from prison populations, administer the chemical to them, and determine its effects on the human body. Or a psychologist studying the effects of extreme variations in climate on the human body may subject consenting prisoners to such variations and test their reactions. Though such experiments are usually very carefully designed to minimize the risk to participants, an element of risk always remains. The participants may become ill or even die of unexpected physical or emotional effects. Because of this danger, volunteers are usually promised special privileges during the course of the experiment and even a reduction of their prison sentences. In cases involving unusual risk, full pardons may be promised. Is it ethical to use prisoners for such experiments? Is it ethical to provide such inducements to volunteers?

13. Sometimes medical school professors encourage their students to volunteer for research experiments. (Student volunteers are used just as prisoner volunteers are, though without rewards—except, of course, the emotional satisfaction of having contributed to progress.) Is such encouragement ethically permissible?

14. Some geneticists, notably Dr. Herman J. Muller, a Nobel Prize winner, have proposed that sperm banks solicit donations of sperm cells from carefully selected men whose lives had shown unusual mental, emotional, or physical gifts. Couples would then be able to select the genetic material of their choice and therefore produce a child endowed with the heredity that matched their ideals. Evaluate the morality of this proposal.

15. The transplants of organs such as the heart and the kidneys have been shown to be possible. Before too long, scientists assure us, the transplant of the brain will also be a reality. Will such an operation ever be ethically justifiable? In answering, be sure to consider the various activities of the brain and their influence on personal identity.

16. *Cloning* is making carbon copies, genetically exact duplicates, of individual organisms. It was first developed in the early 1960s by Cornell University Professor F. C. Steward, who agitated carrot root cells, causing them to divide and multiply. Eventually he was able to prompt a single cell to develop into a fully-grown carrot plant. Later, Professor John Gordon of Oxford University achieved similar results with a frog. The possibilities of using this technique with animals—for example, beef cattle—and with humans are very real. There are, of course, technical difficulties that must be resolved. But no knowledgeable person doubts that these will eventually be resolved. When this happens it will be possible to scrape a cell from a person's hand and create an exact copy of that person, a flesh-and-blood replica with the same genetic traits. (The procedure would be to destroy the nucleus of an egg cell from a donor and insert in its place the nucleus of any cell of the person to be copied. After being nurtured in a nutrient medium for several days, the egg would then be implanted in the uterine wall of the mother.) Thus there could be an unlimited supply of Meryl Streeps, Sylvester Stallones, and Michael Jordans. Since heredity is only part of the influence on people, their behavior and interests would not necessarily be the same. But their appearance and basic capacities would be. Discuss the morality of cloning.

17. Hans Jonas has suggested that in considering the ethical character of scientific experiments we should distinguish between "averting a disaster" and "prompting a good."[3] In the first, where the goal is *saving* society, Jonas concedes that extraordinary means may be used. However, in the latter, where the goal, *improving* society, is less urgent, such means may not be tolerated. According to Jonas,

Our descendants have a right to be left an unplundered planet. They do not have a right to miracle cures. We have sinned against them if by our doing we have destroyed their inheritance—which we are doing at full blast; we have not sinned against them if by the time they come around arthritis has not yet been conquered (unless by sheer neglect). And generally, in the matter of progress, as humanity had no claim on a Newton, a Michelangelo, or a St. Francis to appear, and no right to the blessings of their unscheduled deeds, so progress, with all our methodical labor for it, cannot be budgeted in advance and its fruits received as a due. Its coming about at all and its turning out for good (of which we can never be sure) must rather be regarded as something akin to grace.

Would Jonas's distinctions be helpful in evaluating any of the preceding cases (1–16) in this section? Explain.

18. David D. Rutstein made the following assertions about the selection and design of scientific experiments. Do you agree with these assertions? Do they have special application to any of the preceding cases (1–17)? Explain.

    a. "In selecting a question for human experimentation, the expectation of benefit to the subject and to mankind must clearly far exceed the risk to the human subject."[4]

    b. "It may be accepted as a maxim that a poorly or improperly designed study involving human subjects—one that could not possibly yield scientific facts (that is, reproducible observations) relevant to the question under study—is by definition unethical. . . . Any risk to the patient, however small, cannot be justified. In essence, the scientific validity of a study on human beings is in itself an ethical principle."[5]

19. Given the threat that nuclear weapons pose for humanity, is it ever morally acceptable for scientists to engage in research and development work on such weapons? Discuss the conditions, if any, under which it would be acceptable.

☐ War

  1. Do citizens have a moral obligation to serve their country when it is at war? Under what circumstances, if any, is it ethical for a person to refuse to serve?

2. Israel's invasion of Lebanon in 1982 was conducted to root out the PLO forces that had been responsible for terrorist attacks on Israelis. The Israeli action was controversial because the Lebanese people who were killed or whose homes were destroyed during the invasion had done nothing to Israel. Some people argue that it is always immoral for a nation to invade a neighboring nation that has given no provocation. Others disagree, claiming (as the Israelis did) that an invasion is justified if there is no other way to overcome terrorist forces who have set up headquarters there. Which position do you endorse and why?

3. Is it morally wrong for the government to prosecute a person who fails to register for the draft?

4. A growing number of people today believe that war is always wrong, that no circumstances ever justify one nation's taking up arms against another. Is the view ethically sound? In answering, be sure to comment on the questions of a country's defending itself against aggression and of a strong country's coming to the aid of a weak country that has been attacked unjustly.

5. A soldier's thinking about war may change during his service. For example, after experiencing his first real battle and seeing human beings lying dead or in the agony of pain, a soldier might be prompted to embrace pacifism and request discharge or transfer to a noncombat unit. Such a request would not be looked on favorably by his superiors and would usually be denied. Since the man had accepted training as a combat soldier, they would reason, he would be obligated to finish his term of service. Is this reasoning morally sound? Would it be morally acceptable for the soldier to continue fighting, even though he objected to it on principle?

6. A career officer may not object to war in general, but may, after much observation and evaluation, conclude that his or her country's involvement in the particular war of the moment is morally unjustifiable. Would any circumstances make it morally acceptable for the officer to continue to serve in that war? Explain.

7. In the United States, Congress alone has the power to declare or end a war. The president, as commander in chief of the armed forces, therefore has the legal obligation to keep Congress informed of his dealings with foreign powers, particularly during wartime. Are there any circumstances in which it would be ethically justifiable for the president to conduct secret talks with the enemy and with interested third parties in order to set up the conditions for peace? Would any circumstance justify the president's lying to Congress? Explain.

8. Over the centuries the experience of war has produced many "conventions," humane rules to limit the devastation and suffering that conflict brings. One of the foremost of these rules is that only military targets will be attacked: that civilian population centers that contain no significant deposit of war supplies and machinery will be spared. However, during World War II the United States firebombed the German city of Dresden, dropping thousands of tons of TNT and killing more than 100,000 noncombatants. That target was allegedly selected precisely because it was a civilian target and its elimination would demoralize the enemy and, as a result, shorten the war. Discuss the morality of the bombing of Dresden.

9. Guerrilla warfare consists of terrorization tactics designed to demoralize the enemy and thereby achieve the enemy's defeat. Through threats of harm to themselves and their loved ones, civilians are coerced to harbor guerrillas in their villages and to aid them in acts of sabotage. Is it ever ethically justifiable to conduct guerrilla warfare? If so, in what situations?

10. During the Vietnam War reports from North Vietnam claimed that the United States was engaging in the deliberate bombing of the 2500-mile network of dikes that protect countless farms and villages from the flooding of the Red River. The U.S. government denied the charges, explaining that any such bombings that may have occurred were accidental. Were such bombing done deliberately, it would have had several obvious consequences. It would have threatened the food supply, the homes and factories, and the lives of tens of thousands of civilians. It would also have hindered the North Vietnamese war effort, prompted them to be less demanding at the conference table, and perhaps hastened the end of the war. Would it have been a morally acceptable policy?

11. The argument that has underlain many of the wartime atrocities that people have perpetrated is "they started the war, so we're justified in using whatever means are necessary to finish it." A variation of this, which is used whenever it is not clear who "started it," is "they violated the human convention first so we have a right to also." It was used in the Indian wars (though objective scholarship has shown that much of the savagery that was attributed to the Indians was done first by whites). It was used during World War I and World War II. It was used in Korea and Vietnam. Evaluate the argument from an ethical standpoint.

12. The practice of torturing prisoners to obtain military information is as old as the art of war. Captives are beaten, subjected to electric shock, made to go without sleep for days, and given little or no food. Is such treatment ever justifiable? Be sure to consider unusual situations as well as more common ones—for example, the situation in which the captive is a guerrilla who, there is reason to believe, may have poisoned a city's water supply or placed a time bomb in a public area.

13. Anticipating the possibility that their soldiers may one day be captured by the enemy, some modern armies include in their basic training exposure to torture techniques. That is, they subject their own troops to mild forms of torture in order that they may learn how to resist torture. Is this practice justifiable morally? If you believe it is justifiable only under certain conditions, specify the conditions.

14. Like every aspect of modern existence, the waging of war is largely technological. Among the weapons now available are bombs that seek out groups of people (presumably the enemy) through heat sensors and fragmentation bombs that burrow into the earth to await detonation when someone (presumably an enemy soldier) steps on them. Are such weapons morally legitimate in war? Explain.

15. The Pentagon has spent millions of dollars for research into "electro-optical warfare." The device that was the subject of much of this research is the versatile laser beam. It has the potential for use as an ICBM interceptor. Traveling at the speed of light, it can catch and explode the most sophisticated missiles an enemy might launch. It can ignite wooden targets miles away and can instantly burn out the eyes of anyone who looks directly into it. When aimed at an enemy soldier, it can unerringly burn a fatal hole in his body.[1] Is research into the use of such weapons ethically justifiable? Is the use of such weapons any less moral than the use of guns?

16. If such weapons as those discussed in the preceding question become a reality, would it be morally wrong to work in a company that makes them? To hold stock in such a company?

17. Another avenue of potential for warfare is meteorology. Scientists agree that we presently have or will soon have the technological ability to change the earth's temperature, cause tidal waves, create "holes" in the atmosphere that would permit harmful solar radiation to shower selected geographical areas, and create precipitation where we wish. (There have been reports that the last potential was actually realized by the United States in the Vietnam War to impede travel along the Ho Chi Minh trail.) Comment on such practices from an ethical standpoint.

A SUGGESTION FOR FURTHER STUDY

Many times students will complete an enjoyable college course with a firm resolution to continue studying the subject on their own. Yet somehow, despite their good intentions and their genuine interest in the subject, they never get around to keeping their resolution. The reason is usually that they think of further study in terms of buying or borrowing a book. But which book? They don't know and they don't know how to find out because they are not sure whether they want a general history of the subject, a discussion of one particular aspect of it, a treatment of contemporary issues, or a biography of a famous contributor to the subject.

If you are now making such a resolution about the subject of ethics, here is how to be sure you keep that resolution. Make it very modest. Instead of resolving to buy or borrow a book, resolve to read a single *article* the next time you visit the library and have a few spare minutes. To find the article you want, you needn't search through the magazine index or browse through current periodicals. All you have to do is consult one of the following works:

> *The Great Ideas: A Lexicon of Western Thought,* by Mortimer Adler (New York: Macmillan Publishing Company).

Adler, the author of dozens of scholarly books, is one of the foremost authorities on the history of Western philosophy. Unlike most of his works, *The Great Ideas* does not argue for any particular perspective but recounts, in a nonpartisan manner, what significant thinkers have said about 102 subjects from "Angel" to "World." The essays cover most major topics related to ethics, including "Courage," "Desire," "Duty," "Good and Evil," "Justice," "Prudence," "Temperance," and "Virtue and Vice."

If this book is not available in your library, look for the larger companion work, *Great Books of the Western World* (of which *The Great Ideas* was originally a part). The Great Books collection includes selections from 434 works by 73 authors. An unusually thorough indexing system, called the *Syntopicon*, enables the reader to find what any of these authors had to say about the most specific aspect of a subject—for example, what thinkers from Plato to Freud had to say about "the relation between love and friendship."

Encyclopedia of Philosophy, eight volumes (New York: Macmillan Publishing Company).

This resource contains numerous authoritative articles on all aspects of ethics (as well as articles on other philosophical disciplines). You may wish to begin with an article about one of the great issues in ethics—for example, "Conscience" or "The Good" or "Happiness." Or perhaps you would rather learn more about the schools of ethical thought. In that case, you would choose an article like "Deontological Ethics," "Teleological Ethics," "Hedonism," or "Utilitarianism." You will also find individual articles on all the great ethicists from Socrates to the present. Finally, you might choose to read one or both of the two detailed survey articles, "Ethics, History of" and "Ethics, Problems of."

At the end of each article is a bibliography of works that provide even more specific and detailed information on the subject of the article. Most of these books will either be on the shelves of your college library or obtainable through interlibrary loan. If you have the time to read one or more books, you can pick them up or order them while you are in the library. If your schedule does not afford you that kind of time, you can at least return again and again to the *Encyclopedia of Philosophy,* thus ensuring that your knowledge of ethics will continue to grow long after your formal course in ethics has ended.

WRITING ABOUT
MORAL ISSUES

The principles that apply to writing about moral issues are the same ones that apply to all expository writing. However, because moral discourse often involves the expression of ideas that readers may be inclined to disagree with, sometimes vigorously, there is a special reason to express the principles thoroughly and thoughtfully. In this kind of writing, where persuasion is the main intention, there is no margin for carelessness.

The fundamental principles may be stated briefly: The main idea must be clear, the relationships between sentences and paragraphs must be coherent, the space assigned to each part of the presentation must match the relative importance of that part (in relation to other parts), all interpretations and judgments must be sufficiently explained and supported to satisfy the critical reader, and the overall style must be readable (if possible, *pleasurable* to read).

Let's examine these principles closely, concentrating on the strategies that will help you achieve each one in your writing.

☐ HOW TO MAKE THE MAIN IDEA CLEAR (CLAR)

In most papers about ethics the main idea will be the writer's judgment of the morality of the action that is being considered. Lack of clarity in the main idea usually occurs because the writer began without knowing exactly what he or she wanted to say, hoping to discover the idea in the process of writing. Sadly, the writer will often reach the end of the piece without having made that discovery. Even when the writer is lucky enough to do so, perhaps midway through the piece, by that point he or she has usually confused the reader and made one or more statements that are inconsistent with the main idea. In such cases the reader is apt to dismiss the writer as confused or uninformed. You can prevent this development in your own efforts by scrupulously following two simple strategies:

1. *Begin writing only after you have determined exactly what you are going to say; that is, after you have decided what your judgment is and what basis you have for making it.* This strategy does not rule out "brainstorming" and "freewriting."* In fact, it is perfectly compatible with them, as long as they are used as *preliminaries* to formal writing and not as formal writing itself. If you use brainstorming and freewriting—and they are well worth using—be sure to resist the temptation to deceive yourself by saying, "These notes look good enough to submit as they are; I'll just copy them over to make them neater and the job will be done." Instead, when you have finished producing your ideas, review the ideas and ask yourself what you really want to say.

2. *Experiment with different ways of expressing your main idea and select the best one.* Don't settle for your first way of expressing the idea. That way may lack the qualifications and the exactness that reasonableness demands. As you try different ways of expressing the idea, look at the related ideas and evidence that your preliminary work produced. Ask which way of expressing the thought is most reasonable and best reflects the relevant moral principles that are involved. Ask, too, what your readers' reactions are likely to be, particularly what objections they might have. Refine your statement of the idea in light of these considerations.

---

*These techniques consist of letting your mind range over the subject (or forcing it to do so), without evaluating the ideas that occur, screening any out, attempting to organize them in any way, or correcting your errors. The aim of such techniques is to produce a large body of ideas from which you may *later* select the best ones, the ones you wish to include in your final piece of writing. The principle that underlies brainstorming and freewriting is that ideas and associations will flow best when they are uninterrupted by analysis and judgment.

☐ How to Keep Sentences and Paragraphs Coherent (COH)

You will already have taken one step toward achieving coherence when you determine your main idea. The very fact that you have that idea before beginning will provide a center to your piece of writing, something to relate the other parts to. Yet there are specific strategies you can use to increase the coherence of your writing even more.

1. *Plan the piece before you write it.* The easiest way to plan is to develop an outline. This does not necessarily mean using Roman numerals, capital letters, and so on. (Of course, if you feel comfortable using them, then by all means do so.) It means arranging the ideas that will appear in your paper, deciding which will come first, which second, and so on. The easiest way to do this is to study the ideas you have on your rough-idea sheet and *number them in the most effective order.* The following guidelines will help you decide what that order is:

   The introduction to your paper should identify the essential features of the issue and present a careful statement of your judgment.* If possible, this should be done in an imaginative way that arouses reader interest and creates a positive impression as it informs.

   The body of your paper should develop and support your judgment, presenting the various considerations that underlie that judgment and discussing the various questions and objections that might occur to critical readers. Useful patterns of organization for the middle of the paper include *time order* (you might, for example, discuss the effects of an action in the order in which they would occur in time), *order of complexity* (simpler considerations first, followed by more complex ones), and *order of importance* (less important considerations first, followed by more important ones).

   The conclusion of your paper should reinforce the main idea (your judgment). This reinforcement is usually not accomplished by direct repetition (except in rather long treatments—say, more than 3000 words). Instead, you should use a more subtle method, such as the use of an apt quotation or a statement of your own that recalls the main idea without using the same words.

---

*Skilled writers often withhold the complete statement of the judgment until later in the paper, sometimes at the very end, but this approach is not recommended for beginning writers.

2. *Decide what connecting words or phrases will make clear the relation-ships between your ideas, and add them to the numbers on your rough-idea* sheet. The basic relationships among ideas in persuasive writing are *and* relationships, *but* relationships, and *therefore* rela-tionships. These relationships exist whether or not they are expressed. By expressing them, you make it possible for your readers to move from one idea to another without confusion and help them understand your reasoning more easily. To indicate the basic relationships you may use the words *and, but,* and *therefore* themselves or substitute words. Some common substitutes for *and* are *also, first, second, in addition, next, another,* and *finally.* For *but,* you may use *however, nevertheless, yet, in contrast,* and *on the other hand.* For *therefore,* you may use *so, consequently, accordingly, thus, as a result,* and *in conclusion.* Other relationship words that are helpful in making your writing more coherent are *for example* (to illustrate a point), *now* and *then* (to signal a time change), and *similarly* (to compare). At times a single word or phrase will not do, and you will have to add a complete sentence to make the connection clear.

□ HOW TO ACHIEVE EMPHASIS (EMPH)

Emphasis is stress or prominence. A word, sentence, or paragraph has emphasis if it stands out from other words, sentences, or paragraphs in a piece of writing. Not every part is deserving of the same emphasis, so the careful writer controls the placement of emphasis. The following guide-lines will help you exercise such control in your writing:

Assign an important idea *more space* than other ideas. If you discuss three considerations in a moral issue and give each consideration the same amount of space (say, a couple of sentences or a paragraph apiece), the subtle implication to your readers will be that all consid-erations are of equal importance. On the other hand, if you give one consideration more detailed treatment, that consideration will seem more important than the others. The space given to the development of each consideration should not be left to chance; it should be con-sciously chosen.

Assign an important idea *better space* than other ideas. Not every place in a piece of writing carries the same emphasis. Generally speaking, *the end has the greatest emphasis* because whatever is read last will usu-ally be remembered longest. "End" in this context does not mean con-clusion only. It means the final position of any sentence, any paragraph, or any section of a piece of writing (the body, for example). The construction of individual sentences that observe the principle of emphasis may be a little difficult for the beginning writer, but you should be able to make the final sentences of your paragraphs, the final paragraph of your body, and your conclusion more emphatic. *The place of second greatest emphasis is the beginning* because first impressions tend to last. Accordingly, the beginnings of sentences, of paragraphs, or of any section of a piece of writing (the body, for example) are important places. If you have a number of considerations to discuss in the body of your paper, it will usually be possible to use both the beginning and the end positions to achieve maximum emphasis. For example, begin with the second most important consideration, then turn to the lesser considerations, and end with the most important one.

Use repetition, echo words, and underlining judiciously. (Echo words are words that do not repeat what was said, but are so close in meaning that they recall it; *courage,* for example, might be used as an echo word for *bravery.*) The key word here is *judiciously.* To use any of these devices carelessly, particularly repetition, will distract and even offend the critical reader.

☐ How to Develop Your Ideas (DEV)

Developing your ideas means adding more words, lengthening your treatment of the case or issue. However, unlike padding, developing is not adding words just for the sake of adding them. It is *purposeful* enlargement of your treatment, which enhances its persuasiveness by removing any confusion or misunderstanding your readers might experience, by fulfilling their desire to know more about your judgment and the reasoning that underlies it, and by answering any doubts or objections they might have. There are two steps to follow in the development of your ideas:

1. *Look at your rough-idea sheet and determine which of your ideas might be misunderstood or disputed by your readers.* To perform this step effectively, you must get beyond your own perspective. (From that perspective every one of your ideas will seem unquestionable simply because it is your idea.) You must adopt a critical perspective and see your ideas as your readers, who are unfamiliar with them and uncommitted to them, will see them.

2. *Decide which techniques of development will best overcome confusion or answer objections.* The following techniques are especially helpful in a variety of situations:

    Detailed description. This consists of a more specific presentation of the considerations in the case. For example, instead of merely stating that a certain consequence is likely to result, you would show why it is likely and exactly how it would happen, step by step.

    Brief or extended illustration. This consists of offering examples, cases in point, to support your assertions. Instead of saying that the effects of a certain action would be harmful to the people involved, you would give examples of the harm that would (or might) be done. Illustrations may be actual examples that occurred in similar situations or hypothetical examples (plausible speculations).

    Definition. This technique is helpful whenever you are using a term in a special sense or a way that might be misunderstood.

    Comparison. This consists of evaluating the relative strengths and weaknesses of two or more different lines of reasoning about a case.

    Explanation. This technique is useful for answering the questions that you anticipate your readers will ask. Common questions are why you consider a particular illustration typical, why you choose one interpretation over other possible ones, and why you believe that one consideration in a case (an obligation, for example) outweighs all others.

    Tracing and summarizing. These techniques are more commonly used in advanced ethical treatments, but you may find them appropriate to some of your treatments. *Tracing* consists of briefly presenting the historical development of an idea or perspective. *Summarizing* consists of presenting a capsule version of some material that is too long to use in its original form. One of the most common uses of it in ethical analysis is to present the reasoning of ethicists to reinforce your analysis of a particular case.

□ HOW TO WRITE READABLE PROSE (STYLE)

Readable prose is prose that people find interesting, even pleasurable, to read. To some extent interest lies in the taste of the individual reader. What one person finds interesting will put another to sleep. Nevertheless, there are at least three qualities that tend to generate or at least increase enthusiasm among readers, qualities associated with energy and vitality rather than with dullness and monotony. Those qualities are exactness, economy, and liveliness. Here are some guidelines to help you achieve them in your writing.

TO ACHIEVE EXACTNESS

1. Avoid empty or overworked expressions. It is easy to acquire the habit of expressing your thoughts in clichés or in currently fashionable phrasing. To break that habit, take note of your language. If you find it filled with the kind of phrasing you hear many times each day, make an effort to substitute more meaningful phrasing.

2. Prefer concrete, specific terms to abstract, general ones. It is not always possible in ethical analysis to avoid abstraction or generality, but it is important to do so whenever you can. Keep in mind that the purpose of writing in ethics, like the purpose of any writing, is to make your thoughts clear to others, not to befuddle them.

TO ACHIEVE ECONOMY

1. Choose words to communicate your thoughts, not to impress your readers. Many people have the notion that fancy language and jargon will make them seem knowledgeable. The truth is quite the opposite; such language only makes them seem foolish. The right approach was best summed up by the distinguished essayist and novelist George Orwell when he said, *"Never use a long word where a short word will do."*

2. Wherever possible without sacrificing meaning, reduce a sentence to a clause, a clause to a phrase, a phrase to a word. (This does not prevent you from developing your ideas. Development is adding content, not multiplying words unnecessarily.)

TO ACHIEVE LIVELINESS

1. Control the rhythm and pace of your phrasing. Rhythm refers to the melodiousness of your writing, pace to the relative speed at which it moves. By reading your writing *aloud*, you can get a good idea of whether it is lively to read, whether it not only looks good, but sounds good as well. If your writing does not sound good when read aloud, try changing the phrasing of rough passages (to improve the rhythm) and moderating the sentence and paragraph length (to improve the pace).

2. Use vivid language in place of bland, predictable language. This guideline must be used with care, of course. Vividness can add a dramatic quality to your writing that will increase its liveliness, but if you use it carelessly, it will undermine exactness. To use it effectively, be sure the vivid expression does not represent an idea you cannot defend.

3. Vary your sentence style and your paragraph length. The essential ingredient in boredom is *sameness.* By reducing the degree of sameness in your writing, you overcome monotony and increase liveliness. Examine your sentences and paragraphs whenever you write. If the sentence length is unvaried, change it; make some sentences longer, some shorter. If all your sentences begin in much the same way, change the order of phrases or clauses or move an adverb around. Similarly, if your paragraphs are all the same length, and especially if they are all long, your paper will appear monotonous even before it is read. With a little skillful adjusting, you can usually achieve some variety in paragraph length without awkwardly separating related ideas. (A good average length for your paragraphs is ten lines, with variations from perhaps five to fifteen lines.)

One final note. Throughout this section we have been discussing rhetorical principles, but we have not mentioned grammar and usage. The reason for this is not that those concerns are unimportant, but that they cannot be treated adequately in a brief appendix. Critical readers may overlook an occasional lapse in grammar and usage. However, numerous errors will create a formidable distraction and suggest to readers that you are a careless person. Such a suggestion will hardly help your efforts to persuade readers of the soundness of your views. To make the best impression on your readers, see that any grammatical errors are corrected before you complete your final draft. A good dictionary is an indispensable tool for this task.

NOTES

CHAPTER ONE

1. "New Law Sides with Rape Victim," *Oneonta* (New York) *Star,* July 23, 1982, p. 11.

2. GKC, *Orthodoxy* (Wheaton, IL: Harold Shaw, 1994; first published in 1908), 70.

3. Greg Brown, "Mutilated Voodoo Dolls Found in Delaware," *Oneonta Star,* July 23, 1982, p. 1.

4. "Couple Who Let Baby Die Guilty," *Binghamton* (New York) *Press,* May 18, 1982, p. 5A.

5. *Binghamton Press,* August 7, 1982, p. 4A.

6. *Burden of Proof,* CNN-TV, November 30, 1995.

7. "Zoo Kills Two Bears for Lack of a Home," *Oneonta Star,* May 15, 1982, p. 1.

8. "Right to Liberty," *New York Times,* April 25, 1982, p. 49.

CHAPTER TWO

1. *Research on the Effects of Television Advertising on Children: A Review of the Literature and Recommendations for Further Research.* National Science Foundation, 1977, pp. i–ii.

2. *Facts on File:* 1971, Vol. XXXI, No. 1588, p. 248.

3. *Facts on File:* 1956, Vol. XVI, No. 800, p. 68.

CHAPTER THREE

1. Among the books that set forth the assumptions and approaches of values clarification are S. B. Simon and others, *Values Clarification,* revised edition (New York: Hart, 1978); also L. E. Raths and others, *Values and Teaching,* 2nd edition (Columbus, OH: Merrill, 1978).

2. Carl R. Rogers, *On Becoming a Person: A Therapist's View of Psychotherapy* (Boston: Houghton Mifflin, 1961), 22.

3. Ibid., 60–61.

4. Ibid., 119.

5. Allan Bloom, *The Closing of the American Mind* (New York: Simon & Schuster, 1987), 175, 228.

6. *Today Show,* NBC-TV, November 14, 1995.

7. "White Slavery, 1972," *Time,* June 5, 1972, p. 24.

8. Lucy Morgan, "A Funeral Leaves a Town Torn," *St. Petersburg Times,* July 27, 1991, 1B.

9. "Mummy Removed from Public View," *New York Times,* September 10, 1972, p. 42.

10. "He's Cashing in on the Jobless Trend," *Los Angeles Times,* April 21, 1982, Part V, p. 1.

11. "Nassau Officer Pleads Guilty . . . ," *New York Times,* April 18, 1982, p. 45.

12. "Two Accused of Selling Unborn Babe," *Oneonta Star,* July 23, 1982, p. 20.

CHAPTER FOUR

1. T. W. Adorno et al., *The Authoritarian Personality* (New York: Harper & Brothers, 1950), 147–48.

2. Else Frenkel-Brunswik, "Prejudice in Children," *Psychology in Action,* edited by Fred McKinney (New York: Macmillan, 1967), 276–90.

3. Samuel Johnson, quoted in *The Quotable Johnson: A Topical Compilation of His Wit and Moral Wisdom,* edited by Stephen C. Danckert (San Francisco: Ignatius Press, 1992), 39.

4. Elizabeth Loftus and Katherine Ketcham, *Witness for the Defense* (New York: St. Martin's Press, 1991), 57.

5. "Thompson Lauds Grant for Lewdness," *The Denver Post,* September 4, 1995, p. 2A.

6. David L. Wheeler, "Researchers Debate Ethics of Payments for Human Subjects," *Chronicle of Higher Education,* August 14, 1991, p. A7.

7. Douglas Pasternak and Peter Cary, "Tales from the Crypt," *U.S. News and World Report,* September 18, 1995, pp. 70–82.

8. "Priest Picketed for Drowning Cats," *Oneonta Star,* February 19, 1982, p. 2.

CHAPTER FIVE

1. Clyde Kluckhohn, *Mirror for Man* (New York: McGraw-Hill, 1949), 18–19.

2. May and Abraham Edel, *Anthropology and Ethics* (Springfield, IL: Charles C. Thomas, 1959), 88–89.

3. Ruth Benedict, *Patterns of Culture* (Cambridge, MA: Riverside Press; and Boston: Houghton Mifflin, 1934), 45–46.

4. Ibid., 210, 216.

5. Ibid., 130–72.

6. Colin M. Turnbull, *The Mountain People* (New York: Simon & Schuster, 1972).

7. Kluckhohn, *Mirror for Man,* 41.

8. Kluckhohn, *Mirror for Man,* 177–78.

9. Edel, *Anthropology and Ethics,* 88–89.

10. Mortimer J. Adler, *Desires, Right and Wrong: The Ethics of Enough* (New York: Macmillan, 1991), 193–94.

11. Mortimer J. Adler, *Truth in Religion: The Plurality of Religions and the Unity of Truth* (Macmillian, 1990), 156.

12. Cited in Hadley Arkes, "German Judges & Undue Burdens," *Crisis,* July–August, 1994, p. 16.

13. Debbie Taylor, "China Dolls," *Caracas* (Venezuela) *Guardian Weekly,* November 27, 1994.

CHAPTER SIX

1. These examples are taken from the Tao (the "way") in C. S. Lewis, *The Abolition of Man,* softcover edition (New York: Macmillan, 1965), 97–121.

2. *American Sociological Association Code of Ethics* (Washington, DC: American Sociological Association, 1989). Because of the Code's conciseness, eight pages in total, specific page citations are omitted.

3. Mortimer J. Adler, *Desires, Right and Wrong: The Ethics of Enough* (New York: Macmillan, 1991), 13–14.

4. Ibid., 33.

5. Mortimer J. Adler, *Ten Philosophical Mistakes* (New York: Macmillan, 1985), 126.

6. Stephen Burd, "U.S. Won't Back Creation of Human Embryos for Research," *The Chronicle of Higher Education,* December 14, 1994, p. A32.

7. "The Inhuman Use of Human Beings: A Statement on Embryo Research by the Ramsey Colloquium," *First Things,* January 1995, pp. 17–21.

8. Joseph Fletcher, *Situation Ethics: The New Morality* (Philadelphia: Westminster Press, 1966), 44, 39.

9. Norman L. Geisler, "The Collapse of Modern Atheism," in Roy Abraham Varghese, editor, *The Intellectuals Speak Out About God* (Dallas: Lewis & Stanley, 1984), 149.

10. GKC, *Orthodoxy* (Wheaton, IL: Harold Shaw, 1994; first published in 1908), 113.

11. Ibid., 115.

CHAPTER SEVEN

1. Errol E. Harris, "Respect for Persons," *Daedalus,* Spring 1969, p. 113.

2. Geoffrey Edsall, "A Positive Approach to the Problem of Human Experimentation," *Daedalus,* Spring 1969, pp. 470–71.

3. "Selling to School Kids," *Consumer Reports,* May 1995, pp. 327–33.

4. Jack Anderson, "Army Scientists Move Closer to Orwell's 1984," *Oneonta Star,* August 5, 1972, p. 5.

CHAPTER EIGHT

1. W. D. Ross, *The Right and the Good* (Indianapolis: Hackett, 1988; first published in 1930), pp. 20–23.

2. James Q. Wilson, *The Moral Sense* (New York: Free Press, 1993), as excerpted in *Education Week,* September 8, 1993, p. 41.

3. "The AEC and Secrecy," *Time,* August 14, 1972, p. 73.

CHAPTER NINE

1. Mortimer J. Adler, *The Great Ideas: A Lexicon of Western Thought* (New York: Macmillan, 1992), 838–39.

2. Ibid., 110.

3. All examples are from the Council of Scientific Society Presidents, *Society Policies on Ethics Issues* (Washington, DC: Council of Scientific Society Presidents, May 1995), unpaginated.

4. "Hollow Holiness," *Time,* August 14, 1972, p. 45.

5. Deborah Lutterbeck, "No Sacred Cows," *Common Cause Magazine,* Spring 1995, pp. 4–5.

6. Quoted in *The Chronicle of Higher Education,* September 22, 1993, p. B3, from an article in *Harper's Magazine,* September 1993.

7. "Cop Suspended for Nude Photos," *Oneonta Star,* July 31, 1982, p. 9.

8. "Hundreds Reply to Pregnancy Cost Ad," *New York Times,* August 13, 1972, p. 67.

9. "Road to Survival a Gruesome Path," *Oneonta Star,* December 27, 1972, p. 1.

CHAPTER TEN

1. Henry K. Beecher, "Scarce Resources and Medical Advancement," *Daedalus,* Spring 1969, pp. 280–81.

CHAPTER ELEVEN

1. Stanton E. Samenow, *Inside the Criminal Mind* (New York: Times Books, 1984), 180–81.

2. "Mind Hunter," *Dateline NBC,* November 1, 1995.

3. "Seven-Year-Old Boy Charged . . . ," *Oneonta Star,* July 22, 1982, p. 2.

4. "Husband Says Wife Begged for Death," *Oneonta Star,* July 31, 1982, p. 2.

5. "Five Teens Charged in Fatal Derailment," *Oneonta Star,* July 9, 1982, p. 1.

CONTEMPORARY ETHICAL CONTROVERSIES

EDUCATION

1. " 'Lesbianism' Charges Prompt Course Review," *Oneonta Star,* July 19, 1982, p. 2.

2. *New York Times,* November 26, 1972, p. 41.

MEDIA AND THE ARTS

1. Robert M. Liebert and Joyce Sprafkin, *The Early Window: Effects of Television on Children and Youth* (New York: Pergamon Press, 1988), 147.

SEX

1. "Under the Yum-Yum Tree?" *Binghamton Press,* December 12, 1972, p. 1.

2. Boyce Rensberger, "Clinics for Sex Therapy Proliferate over Nation," *New York Times,* October 29, 1972, p. 1.

3. Ibid., p. 66.

4. Ibid.

5. "1986: A Space Odyssey to Mars," *Time,* December 11, 1972, p. 47.

GOVERNMENT

1. "SBA Sex Palace Loan Irks Reformers," *Oneonta Star,* June 10, 1982, p. 2.

2. "U.S. Recruited Nazis in Spy Network," *Oneonta Star,* May 17, 1982, p. 1.

3. George Bria, " 'Tens of Thousands' Are Still Enslaved," *Binghamton Press,* October 28, 1972, p. 4.

4. Walter Sullivan, "The Lady Was 2,000 Years Old," *New York Times,* August 6, 1972, Section 4, p. 9.

LAW

1. "Taser Gun 'Wilts' Feisty Prisoners," *Oneonta Star,* June 26, 1982, p. 1.

2. "The Lawyer of Last Resort," *Time,* May 17, 1982, p. 64.

BUSINESS

1. *Today Show,* NBC-TV, December 2, 1995.

2. "Products Unsafe at Home Are Still Unloaded Abroad," *New York Times,* August 22, 1982, Section 4, p. 9.

3. "U.S. Charges Nineteen . . . ," *Oneonta Star,* June 23, 1982, p. 1.

4. Jack Anderson, "Double Suicide," *Oneonta Star,* November 24, 1972, p. 4.

MEDICINE

1. *Dateline,* NBC-TV, November 1, 1995.

2. "Burn Victim Shuffled for Lack of Insurance," *Oneonta Star,* May 10, 1982, p. 12.

3. " 'Doctor, Do We Have a Choice?' " *New York Times Magazine,* January 30, 1972, p. 24.

4. "Philosophical Reflections on Human Experimentation," *Daedalus,* Spring 1969, p. 244.

5. "Society Speed," *Time,* December 18, 1972, pp. 76–77.

SCIENCE

1. Rick Scott, "Indians Charge Heritage Plundered, Flooded Out," *Oneonta Star,* October 2, 1972, p. 1.

2. Jane Brody, "All in the Name of Science," *New York Times,* July 30, 1972, Section 4, p. 6.

3. "Philosophical Reflections on Human Experimentation," *Daedalus,* Spring 1969, p. 229f.

4. "The Ethical Design of Human Experiments," *Daedalus,* Spring 1969, p. 529.

5. Ibid., p. 524.

WAR

1. "Now, the Death Ray?" *Time,* September 4, 1972, p. 46.

INDEX